NatWest Small Business Bookshelf

This series has been written by a team of authors who all have many years' experience and are still actively involved in the day-to-day problems of the small business.

If you are running a small business or are thinking of setting up your own business, you have no time for the general, theoretical and often inessential detail of many business and management books. You need practical, readily accessible, easy-to-follow advice which relates to your own working environment and the problems you encounter. The books on the NatWest Small Business Bookshelf fulfil these needs.

- They concentrate on specific areas which are particularly problematic to the small business.

- They adopt a step-by-step approach to the implementation of sound business skills.

- They offer practical advice on how to tackle problems.

The authors

John C. Lambden is a graduate of the London Business School and a small businessman currently running several businesses in the antiques, DIY and small business consultancy sectors. He was a visiting Senior Tutor on the London Business School's 'Firmstart' and 'New Enterprise' programmes from 1985 to 1989.

David Targett is a Senior Lecturer in Decision Sciences at the London Business School and is a past Director of the part-time MBA programme. He is author of *Pocket Guide to Business Numeracy* and *Coping with Numbers*. He is currently involved in major research and consultancy projects relating to information technology and distance learning.

Other titles in this series

A Business Plan
Book-keeping and Accounting
Computerisation in Business
Exporting
Franchising
Hiring and Firing
Managing Growth
Purchasing for Profit
Retailing
Selling
Small Business Survival
Starting Up
Understanding VAT

NatWest Small Business Bookshelf

Small Business Finance
– A simple approach

John C. Lambden
David Targett

Pitman ⊞

Pitman Publishing
128 Long Acre, London WC2E 9AN
A Division of Longman Group UK Limited

First published in Great Britain in association with the National Westminster Bank,
1990

© Longman Group UK Ltd 1990

British Library Cataloguing in Publication Data

Lambden, John
  Small business finance: a simple approach. – (Natwest small business bookshelf)
  1. Great Britain. Business firms. Finance
  I. Title   II. Targett, David   III. Series
  338.60410941

ISBN 0 273 03203 8

Typeset, printed and bound in Great Britain

Contents

Preface   vii

Introduction   ix

Part one: Background

Our approach   1   1

The role of banks   9   2

The role of accountants   19   3

Part two: Is the business viable?

Breakeven analysis   25   4

Breakeven analysis in practice   31   5

Breakeven analysis with several products   37   6

Business viability charts   41   7

Handling more complex businesses   49   8

Part three: Will the business survive?

Survivability   61   9

Survivability: the case studies   69   10

Part four: The future

Growth   83   11

Some practical problems of growth   89   12

And finally . . .   101   13

Appendix   109

Index   113

Preface

This book has been produced as a direct result of experiences gained whilst advising small business people on the London Business School's 'Firmstart' and 'New Enterprises' programmes.

We found, for example, that when selecting candidates for the courses, despite interviewing in pairs, our success rate in a 45-minute interview in sorting out the plausible no-hopers from the hesitant genius was hardly outstanding. Simple analytical tools to help the decision-making process were required — hence the need to produce our own. On the other hand we discovered that whilst a comprehension of the 'numbers' was *always* essential to survival never mind success, the vast majority of small business people avoided 'cracking' these numbers like the proverbial plague. The reasons for this were often complex but invariable involved faulty communications between the three key players — the banker; the accountant and the small business person — as well as any technical problems involved in 'doing the books'.

This book is therefore designed not only to improve communication between all parties involved but, perhaps far more importantly, to assist the would-be entrepreneur to find out if they are really on to a 'winner' or 'loser' *before* it costs them anything. It should also enable even the most non-numerate entrepreneur to gain the confidence and techniques necessary to learn how to handle and understand the 'numbers' their business depends on. Hence with insights into both these perennial problems the small business person is thus better prepared to raise the capital their business will need.

Our thanks are due to Don Valentine FCA, for his invaluable comments on the accountancy section and Eric Swidenbank of NatWest for his help on the banking chapter. We are also grateful to Tim Ellis of Bidwell's for producing the excellent software for our analysis of small businesses. Last but not least our thanks to Mary Hardie who managed to both decipher our writing and type the entire manuscript the week before Christmas.

John Lambden
David Targett

April 1990

Introduction

In 1985 the London Business School launched an advertising campaign on Capital Radio for small business people to fill 30 places on the first of its government sponsored 'Firmstart' programmes. The success of that campaign was literally of prize-winning proportions as thousands of people flocked to the various open evenings and hundreds applied for the 30 available places.

As a gross simplification, all these people had five things in common:

- They actively disliked their bank manager and avoided him whenever possible.
- They thought that their accountant (if they had one) had 'ripped them off' if they were charged more than £250 for the year.
- They did not know (even when they had been trading for some time) whether they were making a profit or a loss. Perhaps more painfully when they did 'know' they were often wrong.
- They were all highly committed, hard working and enthusiastic people.
- They suffered from the impression that they were in the middle of a financial smokescreen whilst at the same time thinking that all they really wanted to do was get on with the job.

If any of these five points rings any bells, then this book is for you.

However, no one book could possibly cover adequately all the tasks involved in starting up and eventually running a small business. We have set our sights on the financing task. To help explain what we mean Fig. 1 illustrates our objectives and puts them in context.

This schematic (which does not include all tasks) tells you what the book is about. We are trying to produce a simple picture as to whether the business is a starter or non-starter and then whether it can survive. This reveals automatically whether the business needs finance and in what amounts. Simultaneously we try to remind you of the ever-present personal factors which can render these numbers pointless!

Other tasks, those relating to pre-conditions and detailed planning, will be described in outline but not in detail. Readers will be told where to get help for these other tasks. Not all the topics covered by the book are included in the chapter headings. The book contains

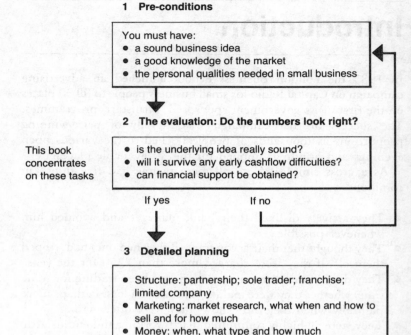

1 Pre-conditions

You must have:
- a sound business idea
- a good knowledge of the market
- the personal qualities needed in small business

2 The evaluation: Do the numbers look right?

This book concentrates on these tasks
- is the underlying idea really sound?
- will it survive any early cashflow difficulties?
- can financial support be obtained?

If yes   If no

3 Detailed planning

- Structure: partnership; sole trader; franchise; limited company
- Marketing: market research, what when and how to sell and for how much
- Money: when, what type and how much
- Professional support: accounting, tax, insurance
- Human Resources: recruiting, employing, managing
- Equipment: purchasing, leasing, type
- Premises: location, how to finance
- Competition: how many, who, can they retaliate

Fig. 1 Starting up and expanding a small business

a wealth of case material which is commented on extensively. These comments pick up a wide range of issues associated with the case. For example, Market Research is not explicitly mentioned as a chapter heading but it is discussed in the context of the cases.

1 Our approach

Theme: Viability = Credibility = Finance

This book is not designed to give anyone a guaranteed method of
raising the money they think they need, nor to list all the places
where finance may be obtained. There are lots of other books which
will do that far better and in much greater detail. NatWest, for
example, with their Business Information Bureau can provide tailor-
made information on grants and government assistance for each
small business person, according to his or her type of small business,
and where it is located. This book is designed for the reader who
is prepared to think, digest and learn from the often painful
experiences recounted in the text. Hence, it is for the vast majority
of small business people who know it is a lonely, worrying and often
nasty world out there. To those 'entrepreneurs' who already know
how to walk on water, have no doubts as to their eventual success
and who are merely seeking to make their first million this week
and not next, we say *Bon Voyage* – this book is not for you!'

Success or failure?

In simple terms, this book is primarily about *whether* you should
raise money rather than about *where* that money comes from. If you
have properly thought through the 'whether' part, the 'where' is
almost a technical matter. The source of the money generally only
assumes nightmarish proportions when you are not clear why you
need it.

Two factors are crucial in determining the success or failure of
a small business. In the long term, the basic underlying soundness
of the business governs its health and growth. The first factor
therefore is whether the nature of the business has the potential to
produce profits. There is no point selling a million pounds worth
of your product if it costs a million and half to make it. In the short
term, the lack of sufficient cash at the right time has caused
fundamentally sound businesses to fail. The second factor therefore
is whether the need for cash, as well as profits, can be met. Hence

the moral of this book: knowing where and how to obtain finance is of limited value if the recipient has little idea how to use it effectively.

This book presents simple methods to carry out the assessment of this effectiveness. The first is *Breakeven Analysis* to test the basic soundness of the business; the second is *Cashflow Analysis* to estimate cash needs. These methods provide a balance between accuracy and simplicity. If they are not accurate enough they will not provide a proper assessment. On the other hand, if they are too complex they will not be understood (while still not guaranteeing accuracy). They are broad-brush approaches, not attempts to produce sets of accounts.

One could argue that the real purpose of this book is to shatter dreams! Not because the authors are natural killjoys (we think!) but because of the terrible necessity to do so before yet more valuable time, effort and, particularly, money is spent fruitlessly.

If you read any small business guidance literature you will find that to be a successful small business person you must be 'very committed', 'hard working' and 'have a firm sense of direction'. The authors' response to this is to point out that all these attributes fit a lemming to perfection. As you know, lemmings are small rodents which every few years leave their traditional breeding grounds in their millions and head along seemingly pre-ordained paths to nowhere. If these paths involve, as they do, running head first off precipices, drowning in rivers or swimming into the North Atlantic then they do it with great willingness and fatal results.

If you insist on jumping off a cliff or taking a one-way swim to corporate death of course we can't stop you. However, we do think it would be a pity to do anything like it accidentally or unknowingly, particularly when an examination of very simple facts in the cold light of day can put a small business person *en route* to either survival (always the first requirement) or prosperous and sustainable growth. If you think we are exaggerating you might think well consider the following true stories.

'I have decided to go into the foreign holiday flat letting business so I've bought an apartment for £30,000 which will bring me in £8,000 a year.'
'How did you work this out?'
'Oh the man who sold me the flat told me so!' (30-year old graduate)

'Your fixed costs are a minimum of 80 K and your sales a maximum of 65 K. We think the council should give your co-operative more money next year.'
(Facts relating to a co-op assembling printed circuit boards by hand)

'Why are you borrowing at 15 per cent and selling to France at 10 per cent margins and then giving them unlimited credit?' (Computer games business with £750,000 turnover after 9 months)

Of course you might well argue that these are extremes. Unfortunately the three stories are from people accepted on the 'Firmstart' programme. Stories from those who were not accepted include such gems as:

'I am divorcing my wife and selling my house to concentrate on my business' (Graduate surveyor)

'What exactly is your business idea so we can assess its potential?' 'I'm not telling you, it's a secret.' (40 + years old 'entrepreneur')

'What I really want you to teach me is how to get rid of the present Managing Director.' (26-year old son of Managing Director)

None of these people were in any way stupid, in fact they were very bright but, like most small business people with limited training, there were some large gaps in their knowledge.

Knowing your business

Your need for relevant information about your business cannot be over-emphasized. Unfortunately this information is likely to be largely numerical and, in our experience, for every would-be small business person who feels perfectly happy with what are quite complex numbers there are 50 who are positively terrified at the prospect of them. They are afraid to an extent which makes them far happier ploughing ever onwards in the dark rather than stopping and working out even the simplest figures. It is these 50, as well as the previous examples, at whom this book is primarily aimed.

First however we need to explain more of the rationale behind our approach. The small business person has at least two major strategic decisions to make. They are *when* to start and *if* to grow. In reality such decisions often come automatically — redundancy, available premises, that really big order — all can swing the hesitant and often part-timer or hobbyist into frenetic and invariably unplanned activity. It is this type of scenario which produces the small business person who has been running a business for some time without really knowing whether it is profitable or not but who never has time to find out! What this book can do *very quickly* is to give anyone in those circumstances a chance to find out, and find out *before* that final decision is made. We would argue moreover that it is also an essential tool for the many people who are determined to make that final decision and do their own thing but can't work out what their own thing really is.

The techniques we use in this book do not guarantee success or failure but what they will do is quantify the type of gamble. For example, every week people can win a million pounds on the pools. This is not an investment strategy to be recommended! Similarly some business propositions can be embarrassingly profitable — a suitcase full of cocaine for example. What this book does is to show you how profitable and how risky your particular proposition is. If, despite bad news, you persist in going ahead — fine, that's your privilege, but we would think it far better if you could change direction slightly and put your undoubted energies into something with better odds.

We would also argue that once you are confident about your chance of success, you are far more likely to be able to sell your dreams to someone else (like your bank manager for example). What is certain is that with some simple numbers to analyse, he is more likely to be helpful than not. This is a logical lead-in to our central premise that:

$$VIABILITY = CREDIBILITY = FINANCE$$

If your business or business idea is viable, you will have credibility; if you have credibility, finance will quickly follow.

The start-up itself is always the most difficult hurdle both financially and psychologically, which is why it covers so much space in this book. However, in terms of risk, it is often the 'shall we grow' time in a small business person's existence which can be the most traumatic, albeit not a possibility that is capable of being understood by those at the start-up stage. In practice most small business people don't want to be millionaires, they just want to be happy. The would-be millionaires, or 'entrepreneurs' as the media would call them, have few doubts as to their destiny and even fewer as to the concept of risk. If you don't believe us, read '*Tycoons*' by William Kay for an analysis of Britain's top millionaires.

Most small business people find their business a perpetual worry – not that they are complaining about what they rightly know is an occupational hazard! However, when it comes to making the leap from the half a dozen employees and sub £250,000 turnover in cheap premises to the expensive lease of a new factory, the quadrupled work force, the £1 million plus required turnover and the overdraft to match, these worries can often reach an unacceptable level. In the second part of the book we can show how to ease some of these worries before deciding whether to make that great leap forward.

However, it is perhaps worthwhile to use a history lesson as the introduction to one of our recurring themes which could be aptly headed 'Look and think before you leap' into small business.

Archimedes was a philosopher faced with the problem of how to determine whether the court jeweller had robbed the King of Syracuse by mixing lead with the gold given to him to make a new crown. As the story goes, the idea for solving the problem came to Archimedes when he was getting into an over-full bath. Like many a good ideas man he then, without a thought for the flooded bathroom, ran down the streets of Syracuse stark naked, shouting the immortal 'Eureka'. Very fortunately for Archimedes his idea was

- right, i.e. it worked;
- as a relative of the King of Syracuse he was both believed and allowed to prove his idea;
- as he was in Ancient Greece he didn't die of pneumonia or get arrested for indecent exposure!

Unfortunately most ideas in modern times do not have such a good combination of circumstances going for them. Unlike Galileo, modern day discoverers will not be tortured by the Inquisition, but life can still seem very discouraging. However, some invaluable pointers can be drawn from this ancient tale:

1. **Test your idea thoroughly** before trying to build a business around it. Whether it be computer software or a steak pie, test it thoroughly on friends and relations first. One's children can be terribly honest – hence useful.
2. **Is there a market?** It always helps to have at least one good customer committed before you go live.

3. **Do the numbers make sense?** In Archimedes' day a grateful King of Syracuse was more than sufficient but it is no point manufacturing your 'wonder widget' if no-one can afford to use it: e.g. a bicycle costing £2000 + which the inventor thought was a product with mass sales potential.
4. **Be prepared.** When you have completed 1 to 3 don't rush to your bank manager or potential customer dripping wet and stark naked.

Official schemes

Now it could be argued that the government Enterprise Allowance Scheme meets many of the above requirements in so far as it supplies an umbrella of £40 per week and access to free counselling services in the first year of start-up. However you must meet the following conditions:

● Have been unemployed for at least 8 weeks and be receiving unemployment benefit at the time of application.
● Be over 18 and under 65.
● Have, or be able to raise, £1000.
● Have opened a bank account in the name of your business.
● Agree to work full time on your business.
● Be based in the UK.
● Have a *new* business; not one which you have been running on the side for some time.
● Have a business suitable for public support: brothel keepers and crack dealers need not apply!

You attend a one-day Awareness Course when your application has been received and you receive at least one follow-up visit by a counsellor during the year. Moreover, acceptance does give you credibility with the banks, most of whom normally grant a £1000 overdraft for a year in addition to the £40 per week. Unfortunately the quality of the advice is like the proverbial curate's egg, 'good in parts', which implies that it is rotten in others. Hence if you are young, with limited capital or borrowing power and eligible for the scheme, we would advise you to apply. However, it may turn out to be of limited practical use. This, in general, applies to many other schemes run by local councils and other bodies. Of course there are many first-rate counsellors about but how can you judge the quality of any advice if you don't know the basics yourself? You can't – so read on!

It is at this stage that we think it necessary to discuss the other two key 'players' in the small business finance game — the banker and the accountant. Often faulty relationships with these two people alone can cause untold harm to small businesses. Our account is intended to dispel some of the myths and enable a good (and necessary) relationship to be formed (or restarted).

1

2 The role of banks

Theme: Knowing how to handle banks and bank managers

Most people think that a bank is a bank and that a bank manager is a bank manager. In practice the major banks vary and so do the personal styles of branch managers, so don't be surprised at the different treatment you receive in a branch only a few miles away from your own. Consequently this chapter could not be based on a particular bank or branch and does not reflect the policies of any one of the UK's major banks.

Research commissioned by a major bank indicates that 50 per cent of small businesses borrow money to start up (no, we don't know any of the other 50 per cent either). Consequently, we think it makes sense to introduce the role of the bank, which is often a critical one at this early stage. This is particularly the case since we find, in practice, that there is more misunderstanding in this area of finance than all the others combined, with the possible exception of how to find a good accountant!

You may have spotted someone leaving a bank with a look of astonishment. It may well have been a small business person who had just paid a first visit to that bank. What could have been the reasons for their feelings? After all, the advertising message of most banks is that they are interested in small businesses and treat them with sympathy and care.

Perhaps the first surprise was some of the bank's small business brochures. They were concerned with rather sophisticated operations with examples such as: 'Rupert had been working in a senior position with a merchant bank for about ten years and was now setting up his own technology consultancy for which he needed to borrow £2 million . . .' Not only did this bank seem to think small businesses had to be sophisticated, they also seemed to think they should not be too small. The brochure went on to ask a potential borrower for complex financial information. Someone in the bank's outer office advised that specialist financial advice could be purchased in order to draw up a business plan. Perhaps only accountants should run small businesses?

The second surprise came with the interview with the bank manager. Among the questions asked, the most important seemingly was: 'Do you own your own house?' There were other understandable questions about personal integrity but the business itself did not appear to be as important. The bank manager seemed much more concerned how a loan would be paid back if the business failed than with the prospects for success and greater future involvement with the bank. The manager said that a professionally prepared financial plan would be welcomed, but did not say how it would affect his or her decisions.

In fairness whilst this situation is unlikely to occur as frequently as it once did the situation is still such that, in general, financial institutions tend to adopt two diametrically opposed approaches to assessing small businesses. The first is to take the standard financial and accounting techniques used for medium and large businesses and apply them to small ones. Mostly the techniques do not work properly when transferred – it is a mistake to think of small businesses as scaled-down versions of large ones. It is also a mistake to think of small businesses as highly sophisticated operations. When a brochure describes a situation like Rupert's, the typical small businessman or woman not only cannot identify with the problem or the services being offered, but is immediately and often severely psychologically depressed at his or her prospects of success *vis-à-vis* Rupert's.

The second and very different approach that banks are prone to use, is to assess the person not the business. While it is, of course, relevant to consider the person running the business, there are other issues than whether he could be forced to sell the family home in order to pay back the loan or whether he wears a suit and tie when he visits the bank manager. Personal qualities and the ability to make a business work are often critical, but their assessment is a subjective matter. What is needed is objective but simple methods for assessing small businesses, at least to filter out those where success or failure appears certain. What we are trying to do with this book is to give you the tools to make the average bank manager or investor feel confident and reassured. This firstly requires numbers which the bank manager understands and you can explain in roughly 30 minutes. This requirement will be discussed shortly but it is perhaps wise to discuss what sort of strange creatures bank managers are and what makes them tick.

How a bank is organised

Assuming that most people never see their bank manager and are quite content to use counter staff to sort out any queries with their ordinary accounts, holiday currency, etc., it perhaps makes sense to explain some simple facts about a typical bank's organisation and how it might affect the small business person.

The first thing to remember is that the branch that you use can be any one of three different types. It can be a sub-branch, a branch or a major branch. The sub-branch, or 'link' branch, is never likely to have a 'bank manager' available to see you. You are more likely to see an 'assistant manager', whose lending freedom will be strictly limited and whose experience and expertise in small business is likely to be equally so. He is, therefore, not the person you should see.

The average high street corner 'branch' or 'lead' branch typically will have, at best, two managers and two assistant managers. In general, the branch/bank manager is likely to be the manager with the greatest experience in handling customers similar to yourself and will certainly have the authority to lend up to £50,000+ on his own authority. However a little market research amongst other customers you know personally may well be helpful in locating the manager with whom you are likely to get on.

If, however, the bank you use is one of the new large regional branches, there may well be a specialist 'Manager – Small Business' or 'Small Business Advisor' who should have been specially selected and trained to handle prospective customers such as yourself. In this situation you will not have a choice if you wish to remain at that 'branch'. Whichever type of branch you deal with, having established the 'right' person, make an appointment for at least a week in the future.

On the subject of 'Small Business Advisors', at NatWest this is an important part of the bank's strategy. Research showed that there was a 'fear factor' with start-up businesses which, in their early development stages, felt overpowered in seeing a more senior manager. Therefore the Advisors are quite deliberately younger and more junior members of the management team. The SBA will not complete business plans or cashflows for businesses, but will assist new starters in the processes they need to go through and, importantly, provide a link with other support agencies such as accountants or solicitors.

Whoever you deal with, there are several very important things to remember about bankers.

Bankers are busy people

They are *very* busy people. Hence you are likely to have no more than three-quarters of an hour to explain your business ideas and secure their understanding and positive support. For the same reasons, being late for your appointment is not a good start.

Bankers are salespeople

One of the commonest misconceptions about banks and bank managers is that they are perceived as equivalent to solicitors, accountants and other 'professionals'. In reality they are retailers, selling money and financial services at increasingly small profit margins as competition gets fiercer, especially now from the Building Societies and foreign banks. It is a tribute to their historically successful selling techniques that

- we don't recognise them as simple salesmen and treat them accordingly; and
- with the exception of British Telecom, they are one of the few organisations who can charge the customer fees after the event without much chance of a comeback.

Bankers and risk

On the other hand bankers would make life far easier for themselves (and in the long run their customers) if they shattered one of the other common misconceptions which is that the money they lend you costs nothing. Whilst it is true that much of the money lent comes from those curious people who leave money in their current accounts (hence lending money for nothing to the bank who is 'looking after it for them'), in practice banks *buy* all the money they lend to the small businessman. This is because even if the money comes from current account balances the banks can and do lend it to others. They could, for example, lend it to the government by buying government stock rather than lending it to the no-doubt deserving small business person.

Why don't they? To some extent they do but the reasons are very important for the small business person to grasp since they lead conveniently into the concept of risk and return. It is essential that every small business person understands the principles of risk and return, particularly when borrowing money. Or, perhaps more importantly for their own well being, he or she should understand why the bank manager or equivalent sometimes declines to lend it.

Bank managers are in the risk business reluctantly. A banker is, like any other sensible person with money to invest, wanting the greatest return for the least risk. Hence, visualise a situation where the government decrees a fixed interest rate no matter to whom money is lent. Would *you* lend money to a small business person when you could lend it to ICI or the British Government? It is unlikely, particularly when in the past banks have not been very good at spotting the successes such as the market trader selling items for one penny in Leeds market who turned out to be Marks & Spencer! Of course the person who invested all his savings in that market trader 30 years ago would now be very rich; merely rich if he or she had invested it in ICI; and positively poor if he had invested all in the British Government (because of the effects of inflation).

However a banker does not invest money in the business, he merely *sells* money to it for a price so he does not, in general, benefit directly, as the mythical investor in Marks & Spencer did, from being your banker even for 30 years. On average, for every £1000 a banker lends Marks & Spencer he probably gets paid £150 (assume bank rate 15 per cent) at the end of the year. For every £1000 he lends a small business person he is likely to get £190. As nine out of ten new small businesses fail, most in the first 18 months and often with bad debts, would you lend to a small business person? Rationally the answer must be no, particularly if you couldn't afford to lose the money.

Fortunately bankers are not unlike good gamblers in that they never 'invest' more than they can afford to lose and, whilst not every market trader will turn out to be a Marks & Spencer and not every horse a Foinavon (100 to 1 winner of the Grand National), both are very happy if their 10 to 1 each way bets come home. So remember, if a bank manager lends you money he has taken a 10 to 1 chance bet on you to start with (9 out of 10 fail!). Moreover, he is only going to get £30 extra for every £1000 lent to you as opposed to Marks & Spencer. It should now be more understandable that banks ask for security and collateral when they say yes, they will lend you those all important few thousand pounds. Because of that security, banks can therefore adopt a more flexible approach to lending to 'risky' potential customers and hence continue the apparently commonsense approach of not 'having all their eggs in one basket'. In practice, knowing whether Marks & Spencer, ICI or whoever is the 'best' investment is so complex as to require massive computers to calculate it, despite very different amounts of dividend paid.

However, certain ground rules don't need computers to be understood and they apply to small businesses as well as big. For example:

1. Hi-tech businesses are high risk (because of constant obsolescence). For example 90 per cent of the present sales of Compaq, a major computer supplier, come from products not existing two years ago.
2. Many industries have economies of scale which make it highly improbable that a small business could survive even with a good product. For example you don't see too many one man band oil refiners or gold mines.
3. Fashion businesses, like hi-tech, are very risky because if you guess wrong you will have spent money on the 'wrong' stock and will have no time (because of long lead times etc.) to get the 'right' stock. Skateboards and Rubik cubes are extreme examples of this phenomenon.
4. Companies making only small profit margins are very susceptible to going from profit to loss. Farmers are a good example where prices are determined by world markets yet local weather conditions can ruin yields in a small area.
5. Management style or lack of it can materially affect whether anyone wants to lend money to a company. The relatively low share price of Lonrho plc is supposedly because of, or despite, the style of Tiny Rowlands, its Chief Executive.
6. Some industries are historically far riskier than others. For example house building, clothing and catering are high up the risk league table. Consequently, even before you have met your bank manager, he/she will already in all likelihood have slotted you into one of these stereotype boxes. Not surprisingly, if you fit into one of the 'bad' ones, you have a far harder job of convincing the bank that you are the exception that proves the rule. Hence the cruel truth that if you are a 'socially committed' would-be manufacturer of 'high fashion' clothing with no credit record and few assets, your local bank manager is unlikely to be of much assistance.

Bankers need clear information quickly

Most people seeing a bank manager do not give a clear, concise, well thought out presentation; even more, they do not present a clear concise written summary of both the main arguments and the main numbers in their presentations. It, therefore, follows that anyone who does both will be well received. Consequently, in the week available to you (remember, you made the appointment for a week ahead) *plan* your presentation. This must include (in written form) both your Cashflow and Business Viability Chart, which can be as simple as the ones illustrated a little later. A written summary of what you are talking about could, for example, be not dissimilar to that used to describe the Market Trader in Case 4. It can contain opinion as well as fact but most importantly it *must be honest*! Bank managers are like computers, they need *all* the facts to analyse correctly otherwise the banking equivalent of 'garbage in, garbage out' could be a rejected request for overdraft facilities but, perhaps more importantly, they could give you the wrong advice. Hence tell him the bad news as well as the good. He or she has, after all, seen hundreds of people similar to yourself and therefore understands the realities of the 'grey' and 'black' economy even if personally not approving!

In addition, please remember to include a brief résumé of what you (and partner/s if applicable) have done since leaving school. It alone can often establish your personal credibility with the bank manager which is an important part of his or her assessment technique.

Another tip is to remember what an overdraft and loan are for. An overdraft is short-term finance and will not be allowed to be higher than stock plus good debtors. Loans, on the other hand, are medium or long-term finance and must be linked to an asset purchase. Hence, don't ask for an overdraft to buy a company vehicle.

Equally, make sure that you ask for the right facility that the bank can offer, normally after direct recommendation or guidance from the bank manager personally. Thus NatWest's 'seed corn' scheme is entirely designed for Research and Development businesses where any pay back may well be several years away. Similarly the merchant banking arm of say, NatWest, would only be involved if the finance required was a minimum of £300,000. A recommendation to NatWest's Growth Options' arm would for example automatically tell you (if you didn't already know!) that your scheme was far too highly geared and hence risky for the generalist bank manager to sanction. Who said 'passing the parcel' was only for Christmas parties!

When all this is done remember to have at least one practice with a volunteer beforehand to establish that your timing and sense are right.

What bankers look for: a summary

1. Your *understanding of your business concept* as outlined in the business presentation or plan and in particular your knowledge of the realities of the market place (e.g. 30-day credit means 45 days!)
2. Your *ability to service the debt* with sufficient reserves for contingencies, i.e. how profitable you will be.
3. Your *level of commitment* as shown by
   - your own money or assets directly invested (which is called equity); and
   - what *you* stand to lose.
4. The *level of security* you can offer, if everything goes wrong.
5. Your *personal track record*, both in business and your personal credit history with the bank.
6. Your *personal approach* in making clear that you are in business for the same reason as the bank, i.e. to make a profit.
7. Your *ability to present and provide information*. Four decimal places in a start-up sales forecast is one example of how to reduce your chances of a loan.
8. Your *personal impression*, physical and mental. So sorry, but the average hippy with 'this great idea, man' is unlikely to receive the greatest welcome from a typical bank manager, particularly if he arrives late.
9. Your *credit rating*. Old county court judgements against you need both settling and explaining.

What bankers will ask of you and what you should ask of them

The bank manager will almost certainly ask you to guarantee your business overdraft facility, normally with a second charge on a property but the absence of this does not necessarily mean an automatic no. Evicting small business people and their families from the family home is not good public relations. Whilst it should be remembered that the bank will go (rightly) to this length if they are convinced that the business failed through criminal negligence, in general the security is more a request for you to prove your commitment and hence encourage you to succeed, rather than to indicate any lack of faith on the bank's part. On this subject you will find that many reference books emphasise that you should not give this very security requested. This is commendable but if you want the money, particularly if the amount is over say £5000, you really will have little option but to give either personal guarantees or allow the bank a 'charge' on an asset, usually your home.

More importantly, whilst your cashflow should indicate clearly what help in overdraft terms you require, always remember that the cashflow is only an estimate. It is far better to ask for an extra couple of thousand pounds over and above what you think you will really need to allow for; that postal strike, major breakdown or other 'act of God' which is bound to happen when things are really tight. After all, you are only asking for more of what the bank manager is trying to sell.

Equally, often forgotten, is asking the bank manager how much he is going to charge your business for this facility. In practice, this area of a bank's lending behaviour can make witchcraft rituals appear quite straightforward. Do not be put off. Your bank manager should be able to tell you exactly how your bank charges are calculated and what interest rates will be charged. Interest rates are based on the expression 'so-many per cent over base'. *Base* is the rate at which the banks themselves borrow money from the Bank of England, i.e. the bank rate. Not surprisingly the rate charged with security is less than when no security is required. If, however, the rate offered is more than '4 per cent over base' with security and '6 per cent over base' without, then either

● shop around; or
● more importantly, ask why your bank manager, to whom you have just given a professional presentation, thinks your business proposition is so much more risky than the normal small business.

Bankers sometimes turn you down

If you are turned down it is likely to be for one or a combination of the following:

1. Business idea considered fundamentally unsound in principle. A national newspaper/magazine launch with less than £100,000 of capital has to be such an idea.

2. Business idea considered too risky. As an extreme: I've got this great tip for the Derby!
3. Insufficient collateral. This is 'Catch 22' when you are just starting, particularly if young. A bank manager must be satisfied that he can get his money back, even if the business fails. Without a house or equivalent how does a start-up get over this hurdle?
4. Security, by itself, is not sufficient without the financial commitment of the borrower. A housewife starting a pin-money type business and borrowing against the family assets would be a good example of this.
5. The business plan or equivalent information is either inadequate, fudged or unrealistic. Most start-ups overestimate sales and underestimate costs and then 'adjust' the figures to give the picture they think the bank manager wants to see. Not all are fooled.
6. The purpose of the loan is not clear, or is only too clear: perhaps to enable the payment of a large salary to be continued.
7. You may find that the lender and yourself are unable to strike up a working relationship.
8. You (and/or spouse) will not sign the necessary guarantees. Whilst most small business advisors advise you *not* to sign this or that guarantee, in practice you sign or you don't get!

Has any of the above happened to you? Don't despair, because the rest of the book should make you adopt a different and more successful approach. Remember the comment about picking accountants? Let us next consider that very problem.

3 The role of accountants

Theme: How accountants can help you

For reasons that are invariably obscure in every specific case, accountants come a safe, if not close, second to bank managers in the small business 'pet hate' stakes. However, faulty communication seems to lie at the base of many problems. To illustrate, consider the old joke: a balloonist, finding himself lost in fog, descends into a large field whereupon he sees a man walking his dog. 'Excuse me, where am I?', he shouts. 'In the gondola of a balloon in the middle of a grass field', comes the answer. The balloonist then says, 'You must be a Chartered Accountant'. 'Yes, but how did you know?' 'Because what you told me was impeccably correct and totally useless!' Unfair and unkind possibly, but not without a grain of truth.

Part of the problem may relate to all professionals whether they be accountants, doctors, solicitors or whatever. It is that subtle arrogance which can produce unspoken thoughts along the line of: 'this is technical and as you're not an accountant you won't understand it, therefore, I'll keep it simple by not telling you'. In fairness to accountants we don't think that they are in the same league as some other professions, as recent negligence cases clearly demonstrate. However, with accountants the problem is sometimes exaggerated because the client *doesn't want to know*! This attitude goes back to our comments in the introduction regarding the genuine fear of numbers and related matters which so many small business people have in abundance. Hence the 'dentist syndrome' prevails: 'I know I have to go, but it hurts, so I'll put it off as long as possible'. Typically the small business person arrived once a year at his/her accountant with a large cardboard box full of every conceivable financial document, often in random order, which was handed over with relief. When some months later they received a set of accounts and a 'reasonable' tax demand they were perfectly happy and so when receiving a 'reasonable' bill sang the praises of their accountant accordingly. The advent of VAT has improved this problem since most businesses have to do at least some bookkeeping quarterly to comply with the VAT regulations, although it is still very common. Unfortunately, what they had actually paid for was a bookkeeping service which anyone can provide and often does. Hence the expression 'my accountant does the books'. The sting is quite simple, most *good accountants don't do your books*, they very sensibly leave that to their clerks and computers and then spend their time (and hence yours as you are paying) analysing the accounts produced from these 'books' to enable them to advise you on the best possible financial course to follow.

That (right) course is not necessarily self-evident for the average small business person and when it involves major sales, or purchases of assets, the wrong course can be extremely painful from the tax angle alone. When ownership transfers from one generation to another are involved for example, we would argue that a good accountant or commercial solicitor is essential if the family finances are not to be severely dented.

When does a small business person need an accountant?

Answer: *before* they even start in business. You might think this is commonsense but remember the dentist syndrome. Often, businesses have grown from hobbies and the person concerned cannot conceive that a £1 – 5,000 turnover is anything to bother an accountant about.

In practice such are the British tax laws that they are invariably wrong. For example, David, earning £40,000 a year, is married to Anne who looks after their two children as a full-time housewife in their four-bedroom house with a £50,000 mortgage, in London. After a holiday in South America, Anne decides that she would like to import Peruvian textiles into the UK and sell them at craft fairs to give her a change and to earn some 'pin money'. As often happens, like Topsy, the business 'just grew and grew' and soon she needed to employ a full-time au-pair and move both children into the same bedroom so she could use one room for storage. Soon, despite good profit margins, she had serious cashflow problems because of the length of time between paying for goods in Peru and her eventually selling them in the UK. As all of this was 'black economy' she felt unable to go to her bank manager. Her husband was less than sympathetic as he now had an au-pair to pay, no guest bedroom, even no wife on market days and no extra wealth to compensate. The net result was that Anne closed down her business and got another part-time job to pay for the au-pair.

The following is what *should* have happened. Most accountants charge a nominal fee for the first consultation, if not giving it free. In either event if David and Anne had gone along to a locally recommended accountant he or she should have advised something like this:

- Open a separate bank account (e.g. D & A (Imports)).
- Keep the business in David's name so that Anne can be paid a salary, thus reducing taxable profit.
- Keep a very simple set of books to record costs, expenses, etc.
- Work out a simple cashflow chart to see how much money you require.
- If you 'lend' savings to this account, note it down. It may well be better to borrow money from the bank even though you have enough savings to cover the requirement.
- 'Transfer' the running expenses and purchase cost of the family's second car to the business.
- Buy *Small Business Finance*!

3

The accountant should then have also pointed out:

- Any net losses that this business makes (almost certain in the first couple of years) can be offset against the tax David pays in his job. These losses could well mean for example that David no longer pays any tax at the higher rate (40 per cent).
- Because you are using your house partially for business purposes, I can negotiate with the tax inspector that some of the costs of running the house can be included as business expenses.
- If the au-pair helps in the business (washing and ironing the goods as they arrive for example), much of her wages can also be counted as a business expense.
- Anne's salary should be limited to her tax free earnings allowance.
- Let me advise you on the bookkeeping system, particularly if you are going to use your home computer. The system should be sensible and not over-elaborate and easily understandable by my staff (hence saving you accountancy fees). This should also make it difficult for me to blame your system if there are any delays in processing your accounts.

We don't think you would argue that that accountant has earned his or her, say, £100 consultant's fee and, moreover, has now set David and Anne on a course where they have a chance of surviving, prospering, and *not* divorcing. Convinced? We hope so. Now let us consider how to choose an accountant.

Choosing an accountant

Firstly you have to consider what sort of an accountant. Anyone can call themselves an 'accountant'. What they can't do is put the letters ACA, FCA or ACCA after their name without being either a member of the Institute of Chartered Accountants (ACA/FCA), or the Chartered Association of Certified Accountants (ACCA). Other 'accountants' may have other letters after their name which may for example show that they are members of the Institute of Taxation or Institute of Chartered Secretaries. This does not always mean that they have failed to pass the examinations required for ACA or ACCA at one time or other and it certainly does not mean that their advice is any less effective. Often the contrary is true as, like herbalists, they may have had to build up their business over a long period by word of mouth recommendation.

In any event, personal recommendation from your small business friends and your bank manager should be your prime route to your first accountant. Ring them up and go and see them, having first established that they are *not* going to charge you for your first 'chat' since they, after all, are selling their services to you. If, after half an hour, you are not impressed or just can't stand the person who you are seeing, don't worry. There is always another accountant just like there is always another bank manager who may suit you better on a personal level whilst still giving the same technical expertise. This is important. People in general do not naturally accept advice from people they dislike no matter *how good* the advice.

This is why, particularly at the start-up stage, we would not recommend anyone going to any of the really big national practices. They obviously have advantages over the small firm but, in general, the small client with zero clout is more likely to find the disadvantages; for example, the impersonal approach which is an unavoidable feature of their systems. Remember when they say they have specialist small business divisions that they normally mean small by *their* definitions not yours, perhaps a turnover of £250,000. They are also more expensive than a smaller practice despite protestations to the contrary. Similarly, we don't think that you will find many larger firms giving you the flexibility on, say, three − six monthly interim figures. These can be particularly useful if the business 'takes off' and your gross margins are low. In these circumstances it can be amazingly easy to be doing lots of business and the more you do, the more money you lose. Hence, in conclusion we would say that as with bank managers it's the name on the office door that matters not the name over the front door.

The cost of an accountant

Try to forget how much your accountant is costing you. The important thing is how much he *saves* you. The accountant providing a book-keeping service, doing your annual accounts and quarterly VAT return may well charge you anything from £250 to £500 + a year. A part-time book-keeper could well be of more use to you and give far better value for money as he or she doesn't have the fixed overheads of a firm of accountants. Equally the accountant who completes and audits the accounts when your book-keeper has finished them to the limit of his/her non-qualified expertise may well charge around £2000 and still be a bargain, particularly if he sorts out your personal tax position at the same time as your business's. Hence, whilst a highly specialised accountant could well charge £500 + *an hour* he could be worth every penny, though in all likelihood a small business will seldom, if ever, require this type of superstar. So don't just take the first figure; compare what he saves you with what he costs. If the answer is not positive, try another accountant or perhaps thank heaven for having such a very simple and profitable business.

Alternatively you might ask what you could do to keep your accountancy bills down. Good examples of expensive sins are:

- Keep a cash book but don't add it up.
- Have illegible writing.
- Have hieroglyphic entries on cheque stubs, etc.
- Don't have a separate personal account so all business and personal matters have to be unravelled at length.
- When the accountant asks specific questions, take ages to answer, or don't answer at all.
- Change your mind about accounts despite having formally approved them because you've found another expense bill for £43.
- Have a personal drawing system which is along the lines of an extra £50 when there's an 'R' in the month.
- Have a 'wild' computer or manual system which is not compatible with your accountant's or anyone else's and you're the only person who understands how to access it properly.

● Submit your accounts late and your tax return even later thereby getting both your accountant and your tax inspector irritated with you.

Having explained some mysteries of the banker and the accountant, we hope your confidence about entering small business has been re-established. Therefore, let us try the difficult but totally vital part – the numbers.

4   Breakeven analysis

Theme: A simple method for measuring whether the business is sound?

Most people starting small businesses think their problems are unique. They are not. Most small businesses have similar financial problems, usually involving profit margins, cashflow, debtors, creditors and, often, what appears to be a lack of understanding from their own bank managers and accountants.

As we discussed in the Introduction, compared with some of the banks' alternative investments, under any definition of risk a small business is risky. Your job is to persuade your potential investor that your small business is:

- Less risky than other small businesses.
- 'Worth a flutter as a fancied outsider'.

Breakeven Analysis can help to solve this particular problem and others and so avoid some of the pitfalls which cause the failure of nine out of ten small businesses. It will indicate whether the business is clearly profitable, non-profitable or marginal. It does not, however, show by itself whether the business is necessarily a winner, but it can show if it is a definite loser. The breakeven point is the level of sales (in volume or financial terms) at which sales equal costs. In other words it is the minimum level of sales if a loss is to be avoided and is, therefore, frequently the starting point for an investigation into a product's or company's profitability.

For example, the research manager of a small home computer company has had an idea for a new children's game. He estimates the fixed costs of development at £18,000 and the variable costs of manufacturing and marketing at £5 per game. The selling price is £11 and the company wants to know how many must be sold if it is to be profitable. A breakeven analysis would show that selling 3,000 games would make sales equal to costs. The company would then know the boundary between profit and loss, so that if the company had a guaranteed order for 3,500 from, say, Hamleys then their bank manager would in all likelihood be very happy to do business.

It is necessary first to understand two important terms: *fixed costs* and *variable costs*. A fixed cost has to be paid whatever the level of sales. When you buy a car the purchase price is a fixed cost; the money has been spent whether you use it every day or not at all. On the other hand the amount spent on petrol varies from day to day depending upon how much you use it. This is, therefore, a variable cost. The purchase price, rates and rent for business premises are further examples of fixed costs because whether open or closed, busy or quiet, the same amount still has to be paid. Raw materials and other stock costs however are variable costs since they will vary according to the sales level.

Breakeven Analysis works by first finding the *contribution*, which is the difference between the selling price and the variable cost per unit. In the computer game example the contribution per game is £6 (price, £11, minus variable cost per unit, £5). Second, the number of units that need to be sold if total contribution is to cover the fixed costs is calculated. If 3,000 computer games are sold, the total contribution is £18,000 (3,000 × £6) which is equal to the fixed costs. Hence, 3,000 units is the breakeven point.

So having established the key elements of breakeven analysis, let us look at a practical example.

Case 1: The Fish and Chip shop

Harry is considering buying a Fish and Chip shop and wants to have some idea of its profitability. He has done his homework by spending time observing shop operations and collecting facts and figures. From what he has seen, 5,000 portions of fish and chips per month seems the best estimate of his sales, given an average price of £1 per portion.

The main variable costs are 40p for the fish and 5p for the potatoes for the chips. At first sight it seems that his contribution is 55p (£1) − (40p + 5p) but this ignores several other minor variable costs for cooking oil, salt, vinegar and wrapping paper. Harry estimates that in selling 5,000 portions in a month he will use 20 gallons of cooking oil at £5 per gallon, 10lbs. of salt at 20p per lb., 10 pints of vinegar at 10p per pint, 1,000 newspapers at 1p each and 5,000 greaseproof papers at 2p each.

Fixed costs include rent, rates, fuel and wages (of the staff and Harry himself). From figures given by the vendor, Harry estimates that in total they are £1,200 per month.

What is Harry's breakeven point in terms of portions per month?

What will his profit or loss be if he does achieve his best estimate of 5,000 portions per month?

Solution

The revenue comes from the £1 he would charge.
The variable costs per portion are:

Fish 40p
Chips 5p

Oil 2p $\left(\dfrac{20 \text{ gallons} \times £5}{5,000 \text{ portions}}\right)$

Salt 0.04p $\left(\dfrac{10\text{lbs.} \times 20\text{p}}{5,000}\right)$

Vinegar 0.02 $\left(\dfrac{10 \text{ pints} \times 10\text{p}}{5,000}\right)$

Newspapers 0.2p $\left(\dfrac{1,000 \times 1\text{p}}{5,000}\right)$

Greaseproof 2p

Total variable costs =   0.40 (fish)
          (in £)   + 0.05 (chips)
                           + 0.02 (oil)
                           + 0.0004 (salt)
                           + 0.0002 (vinegar)
                           + 0.002 (newspaper)
                           + 0.02 (greaseproof)
                       =   0.4926

It is important to be thorough and consider all possible variable costs to avoid serious omissions. However it is equally important not to become bogged down in the second and third decimal places which should not be allowed to dominate an analysis involving estimates such as those above. The essence of the analysis is that every *£1 of sales has cost, roughly, 50p* or, in other words, for every £100 taken in sales, the variable costs have been £50, leaving £50 to pay off the fixed costs.

The fixed costs are £1,200 per month. Now the breakeven calculation can start:

Contribution = Revenue − Variable Costs
          = 1.00 − 0.50
          = 0.50

$$\text{Breakeven Point} = \frac{\text{Fixed Costs}}{\text{Contribution}}$$

$$= \frac{1,200}{0.50}$$

$$= 2,400$$

To break even Harry must sell 2,400 portions of fish and chips per month. The analysis can go further since all the data are available to calculate profit for different sales volumes. If Harry sells 5,000 portions his monthly profit will be:

$$= \text{volume} \times \text{contribution} - \text{fixed costs}$$
$$= 5,000 \times 0.50 - 1,200$$
$$= 2,500 - 1,200$$
$$= £1,300$$

If Harry is confident of selling 5,000 portions per month the analysis has confirmed the viability of the business and there is no need for further calculations. If, on the other hand, he suspects that the sales volume will be close to the breakeven point of 2,400, he must consider what needs to be done to make the business more viable – cut costs, increase price, increase volume, etc. In either event, Harry is now in a better position to decide how much he is prepared to pay for the business.

Comment

When buying any business the critical question is what are the *sales* going to be? It is difficult to get costs completely wrong but sales are a different problem, particularly in a cash business where the 'official' books are unlikely to be completely true and can often be very 'grey' if not simply fraudulent. It is not just the fish and chips that might be cooked! It is estimated that over 20 per cent of Italy's total earnings never appear in *any* books for example.

Hence you should check very carefully both before and after the present owner is aware of your real interest. Stand outside the shop for as long as possible and:

● Count how many people go past and what percentage enter the shop. You can then compare these figures with similar shops elsewhere and, if they are similar, make sensible conclusions. Harry could say that if 125 people per day enter the Fish and

Chip shop and if each on average buys two portions, he will sell 5,000 portions per month (125 × 2 portions × 20 working days).

- Consider what sort of people walk past. For example, if you are buying a sports shop and the average person walking past is a pensioner, beware.
- Check for seasonality. There's no point counting people entering a gift shop the week before Christmas if you don't also count in January/February or July/August.
- Assess wealth. If you are thinking of buying an upmarket wine bar, the average working class area is not the place to be no matter how many people pass by on their way to the factory gates.
- Count how many of those entering buy something. Every type of shop has a different profile and Harry can assume everyone who enters a Fish and Chip shop is a buyer but he couldn't if it was an antiques shop or gift shop.

This chapter has explained the basic idea of breakeven analysis and we will now go on to look at some of the practical details.

5 Breakeven analysis in practice

Theme: Some practical hints for carrying out a breakeven analysis

Harry's Fish and Chip shop was a straightforward business. It is not always so easy to carry out a breakeven analysis. Here are some hints to bring you a bit nearer to being able to put together a breakeven analysis for your own business.

Variable costs

Watch out for several different kinds of variable costs, all of which appear in case studies in the book:

- *per unit* costs, such as the raw material cost of each unit of production, e.g. the cost of a portion of fish.
- *percentage of sales* costs, e.g. credit card commission is a percentage of sales revenue.
- *'profit margin'* costs: when it is assumed that the selling price has been set on a cost-plus basis, e.g. the production costs are such that the price is the production cost plus 20 per cent. This approach to costs is necessary when the price is known and one must work backwards to estimate the costs. It's more difficult but it is also a common pricing system in small businesses.

It is also important to distinguish between *true* variable costs and *apparently* variable costs, regardless of accounting treatment. True variable costs differ according to the output. For example, the managing director's salary may be apportioned over several products but it is still a fixed cost. Likewise so-called development costs, such as those of product development, may be apportioned but they are nevertheless fixed costs. As a rule of thumb – if in doubt, treat costs as fixed. This particularly applies to labour costs which should always be treated as fixed costs except in the strangest circumstances – holiday casuals, for example.

Fixed costs

Fixed costs must all refer to the same period: annual and quarterly costs should not be mixed.

Fixed costs that should be spread over a long period of time can be taken as the interest that would be paid on a loan of that size. For example, an investment with a life of ten years can be equated to an equivalent yearly interest on a loan of that amount. Property and cars should be treated in this way. For instance, an £8,000 car intended to last for two years costs £1,200 per year to buy on a bank loan with a 15 per cent interest rate.

The stages of a breakeven analysis

When we tackled the case of Harry's Fish and Chip shop, the calculations were broken down into a number of different stages. If we can recognise these stages and keep them in mind it will help us when we are looking at more complex businesses.

- *Stage 1*: What's the unit price of the product? For Harry it was £1.
- *Stage 2*: What are the variable costs? Harry's totalled £0.4926 which we rounded up to 50p.
- *Stage 3*: What is the contribution?
  Contribution = Price − Variable Costs
  In Harry's case, £0.50.
- *Stage 4*: What are the fixed costs?
  For Harry they totalled £1,200 per month.
- *Stage 5*: What is the breakeven point?
  $$\text{Breakeven Point} = \frac{\text{Fixed Costs}}{\text{Contribution}}$$
  In Harry's case, $\frac{1,200}{0.50} = 2,400$
- *Stage 6*: What is the expected profit?
  This is the profit based on the best estimate of the sales volume.
  Expected Profit = (Contribution × Expected Sales) − Fixed Costs
  Harry expected to sell 5,000 portions per month, so his expected profit was £1,300.

We are now ready to try out some of these hints on a new case.

Case 2: The driving instructor

David is 24 years old, single and living at home. Currently he has a job with the local council as a clerk earning £135 per week but his ambition is to be a driving instructor with his own business rather than working for a large driving school. He knows a new dual control car will cost £8,000 and that he must first pass the advanced driving test which, with tuition fees, will cost £1,500. He also knows that large driving schools charge customers £10 per hour for tuition. Would his own business be viable? Before you do the calculations or look at our answer, take a moment to consider what your instinctive view is.

David has already done some work to estimate the other costs involved.

1. *Car running costs.* An automobile association tells him that average running costs for the type of car he intends using are 10p per mile. Since his car will be working in low gears with heavy handling, he decides to check out the accuracy of this figure. First, the direct costs for 25 miles per gallon at £2 per gallon come to 8p per mile. Second, a 6,000 mile service at £60 gives a cost per mile of 1p. Third, the costs of tyres and other replacement parts come to about £300 per annum which for 30,000 miles is a further 1p per mile. The 10p per mile looks a reasonably accurate minimum figure.
2. *Advertising.* As a one-man operation, David will probably use only the local press. This is relatively cheap, especially since full page spreads are unnecessary for this type of business. A one-eighth page is likely to cost approximately £40 per week.
3. *Administrative costs.* While David is instructing he clearly cannot answer the phone, hence he needs someone at base. Fortunately his mother has volunteered and is content with pay of £30 per week. At this level no tax or national insurance need be paid. Items such as stationery and, particularly, insurance, will cost another £10 per week. All these administrative costs add up to £40 per week.
4. *Depreciation.* The car will have to be replaced every two years (60,000 miles). Allowing for price increases and the trade-in value, a rough estimate of the replacement cost is £8,000, or £80 per week.

If it is assumed that David borrows the money for the advanced

5

driving test and the initial purchase of the car from the bank at, pessimistically, 20 per cent, his borrowing cost is £1,900, approximately £40 per week.

David proposes to work a 30 hour week and charge £7.50 per hour to undercut the large schools. He assumes that each lesson will cover about 20 miles, consistent with 30,000 miles per year (20 miles × 30 lessons per week × 50 weeks per year). What is his breakeven point in terms of one-hour lessons per week? What will be his profit or loss if he works 30 hours per week?

Solution

Follow the six stages of a breakeven analysis.

- *Stage 1*: What's the unit price of the product?
  The Price is the £7.50 he intends to charge per lesson.
- *Stage 2*: What are the variable costs?
  The only variable cost (varying with the number of lessons David gives) is the running cost.
  Variable Cost = £2 per lesson (10p per mile × 20 miles per lesson)
- *Stage 3*: What is the contribution?

  $$\text{Contribution} = \text{Price} - \text{Variable Costs}$$
  $$= 7.50 - 2.00$$
  $$= 5.50$$

- *Stage 4*: What are the fixed costs?
  Fixed costs (per week) are advertising (£40), administration (£40), borrowing (£40) and depreciation (£80). In total they are £200 per week.
- *Stage 5*: What is the breakeven point?

  $$\text{Breakeven point} = \frac{\text{Fixed Costs}}{\text{Contribution}}$$
  $$= \frac{200}{5.5}$$
  $$= 36.7$$

To break even David must give 37 one-hour lessons per week. If David works 30 hours per week he will make a loss.

- *Stage 6*: What is the expected profit?
  This is the profit based on the best estimate of the sales volume.
  Expected Profit = (Contribution × Expected Sales) − Fixed Costs

$$= 5.5 \times 30 - 200$$
$$= 165 - 200$$
$$= -£35$$

The business is likely to lose £35 per week. Worse, this analysis has not included any wage David pays to himself. He should stay with his local council job.

Comment

No doubt your first reaction when reading the solution to this case was 'I don't believe it! After all you see dozens of instructors about'. We didn't ourselves at first until we realised that one of the reasons why you see instructors about at all hours of the day and night is because they *have* to. What's more, unless they work more than 40 hours per week (which many do), they last in the industry for approximately 3 years, until their car packs up. As they have lived on the money they should have set aside to buy a new car (depreciation) they haven't any capital to continue profitably; so they leave the business or start all over again. In either event the moral of the story is that just because there are a lot about don't think they are making a fortune. Mechanics, interior designers, beauty therapists and dieticians are merely a few additional examples of this small business problem. How do you make a good living when you are a one-man band in a labour intensive industry with lots of competition? Answer: there isn't one. Whilst a few make a good living, the majority survive at best.

5

6 Breakeven analysis with several products

Theme: How to carry out a breakeven analysis when the business has many products

Breakeven analysis for the computer game business, the Fish and Chip shop and the driving instructor involved, in each case, just one product. The answer was given in terms of the sales volume of that product. If there are several products this approach is not possible since there is no single sales volume. In such cases, selling prices and unit costs cannot be specified, just total costs. The breakeven analysis must work in a slightly different way. The next case, an antique dealer, is an example of this situation. The dealer sells many different antiques at many different prices and a sales volume would not make sense. Instead, the analysis produces a financial breakeven point in terms of sales.

6

Case 3: The antique dealers

John and Judy were antique dealers for fifteen years before running a village shop for four years. They have now gone back into the antiques business but finances are a problem. In spite of making a good profit from the sale of the shop, they found themselves with less working capital than expected. This is mainly because the costs of renovating the house they bought have been greater than anticipated. As a result, when they recommenced the antiques business six months ago their starting stock was just £5,000 purchased with a £5,000 overdraft from their bank. They have now asked the bank to double the overdraft facility to £10,000, although this amount is a guess and they are not sure what level of overdraft they really need.

Like most antique dealers they buy and sell almost everything, but John and Judy specialise in buying Georgian and Victorian furniture in need of restoration which they then carry out using sub-contract restorers. They sell the furniture through an antiques centre where they rent space for a total of £50 per week. With their £5,000 starting stock they have so far made £7,500 of sales achieving a

35 per cent profit margin on cost, i.e. on average they sell goods for 35 per cent more than they paid for them, including the restoration expenses. However, partly through delays inherent in putting furniture through the restorers, they have run out of money to buy further stock, apart from that coming directly from sales. Hence they need an increased overdraft. They calculate that their living costs are low, reflecting their frugal standards, totalling £10,000 per year which includes running and paying for a suitable car.

In the antiques business, stock turn is a particularly important concept. From the facts, John and Judy's stock turn must be three, assuming the six months' business so far is representative. Sales of £7,500 in six months equal £15,000 in a year with a starting stock of £5,000 and 15,000 divided by 5,000 is three. This is typical of a business of this type. An increased overdraft would enable them to increase their stock to £10,000 which, they hope, would give sales of £30,000 per year, three times the stock. The question is whether this level of overdraft would make the business viable. If not, what level of overdraft do they need?

Solution

This case requires a slightly different approach to the breakeven analyses described in the previous two cases because there is no unit price, all goods sold having different prices. The approach is to calculate the contribution per £1 revenue, not per unit. The breakeven is then expressed in financial rather than volume terms.

This different approach means that the first stage of the six stages of a breakeven analysis is not necessary since we are always looking at the breakeven point relative to £1 revenue. In effect the 'price' is always £1.

- *Stage 2*: What are the variable costs?
  This case uses the profit margin method of finding costs, introduced at the beginning of Chapter 5.
  The profit margin is 35 per cent of cost.
  For each £100 of items bought the revenue will be £135, i.e. each £135 of sales revenue has cost £100.
  Each £1 of revenue therefore has a variable cost of $£\dfrac{100}{135}$

$$= £0.7407$$
$$= £0.74, \text{ rounded}$$

- *Stage 3*: What is the contribution?
  Contribution = Price − Variable Costs
  If sales revenue of £1 has a cost of £0.74, then:
  Contribution = 1 − 0.74 = £0.26.
- *Stage 4*: What are the fixed costs?
  Fixed costs per annum are antique centre rent of £2,500 (£50 × 50 weeks) and living costs of £10,000.
  Total Fixed Costs = £12,500
- *Stage 5:* What is the breakeven point?

$$\text{Breakeven Point} = \frac{\text{Fixed Costs}}{\text{Contribution}}$$

$$= \frac{12,500}{0.26}$$

$$= £48,100$$

To break even John and Judy must sell £48,100 worth of antiques per year. This will give them sufficient contribution to equal their fixed costs. This sales level will require, given a stock turn of three, a stock level of about £16,000 (£48,100 : 3). To finance this they would need an overdraft of £16,000. Even this would be insufficient because of interest charges. Increasing their overdraft from £5,000 to £10,000 will not be enough.

6

- *Stage 6*: What is the expected profit?
  This is the profit based on the best estimate of the sales volume.
  Expected Profit = (Contribution × Expected Sales) − Fixed Costs
  With an overdraft of £10,000, John and Judy could achieve sales of £30,000 and their profit/loss will be:
  Annual Profit = 0.26 × 30,000 − 12,500
  = 7,800 − 12,500
  = − £4,700

The business is likely to lose £4,700 per annum. An overdraft of £10,000 is not what John and Judy want. The bank should analyse the situation and advise what the proper level of overdraft should be.

Comment

The TV series *Lovejoy* did few favours for the antique dealers' image, reinforcing as it did the notion that all antique dealers have merely to cruise round in their Volvos waiting for their 'noses' to lead them to the inevitable bargains, both materially and sexually. In reality, we would recommend anyone to try a January morning at 5 a.m., complete with hand torch at London's Bermondsey open air market as a much needed antidote! The glamour wears off quickly when you haven't bought anything after four hours in the pouring rain and your Volvo has just been towed away or broken into. Here, yet again unfortunately, results come from 99 per cent perspiration, 1 per cent inspiration and probably 40,000 + miles a year in that Volvo.

7 Business viability charts

Theme: How to keep the information used in a breakeven analysis neat and tidy, and hence useful

Even for a business like Harry's Fish and Chip shop, sorting out prices and costs is never straightforward. When cases get more complicated and when you are trying to distinguish between the one-product situation and the many-product situation, it is easy to reach the wrong conclusions simply because of an error in writing down numbers. To reduce the risks of this type of error and to help you collect all the information together, a Business Viability Chart (BVC) should be used in **every case**. It will force you to be tidy when carrying out a breakeven analysis. Figure 7.1 shows a BVC filled in with the information about Harry's business.

The next case involves a lot of different costs and is a further example, like the antique dealers, of a many-product breakeven analysis.

7

Case 4: The market trader

Jane is a 35 years old part-time market trader selling ladies clothes at weekends in an outdoor London street market. During the week she is a mature design student on a course which she started four years ago. She has been a market trader for three years.

She sells from a 6ft x 6ft stall on Saturdays but 12ft x 6ft on the very much busier Sunday, using herself plus an assistant, who is often different from day to day. Jane buys mainly from wholesalers in the Commercial Street area of East London but does some direct buying which can save 25 per cent. She normally buys up to 50 tops, 30 trousers and 20 skirts at a time. However, Jane deliberately limits her lines to four plus one experiment each week, only some of which she has on display; the rest she sells direct from bags to reduce ironing and space problems.

Like most market traders, Jane's business is highly variable because of both seasonality and weather. In January, February and March she takes virtually nothing, with September to Christmas being the

42 Is the business viable?

Please fill in your answers to questions 1 to 6.

1 Do you want to work in terms of units sold or money? If you have one product you will probably choose units sold. If you have more than one product you will probably choose money.

Please tick: Units sold ✓

      Money

2A **Answer this question only if you ticked units sold in question 1. If you ticked money go on to question 2B.**
What is the selling price in £s?
 Please fill in the box.

Price: £ 1.00

What number of units do you expect to sell? (You can choose per week, per month or per year, but whatever time period you choose, you must keep to it for the rest of the analysis).
 Please fill in the box.

Expected units sold: 5,000

Now go to question 3.

2B **Answer this question only if you ticked money in question 1.**
What is you expected sales revenue, in £s? (You can choose per week, per month or per year, but whatever time period you choose, you must keep to it for the rest of the analysis).
 Please fill in the box.

Expected Sales Revenue: £

Now go to question 4.

3 What are the variable costs per item, in £s?
 Please fill in the boxes.

	Amount	Description
Cost 1 £	0.40	Fish
Cost 2 £	0.05	Chips
Cost 3 £	0.02	Oil
Cost 4 £	0.0004	Salt
Cost 5 £	0.0002	Vinegar
Cost 6 £	0.002	Newspaper
Cost 7 £	0.02	Greaseproof
Cost 8 £		

4   What are the costs which are percentage of price or sales revenue?
    Please fill in the boxes.

	Percentage	Description
Cost 1	%	
Cost 2	%	
Cost 3	%	
Cost 4	%	

5   **Answer this question only if you ticked money in question 1. Otherwise go on to question 6.**
    Is there a cost in Profit Margin terms, e.g. when pricing is on a cost plus basis?

	Profit Margin	Description
	%	

6   What are the fixed costs, in £s? Make sure each cost covers the same time period, e.g. weekly, monthly, yearly.
    Please fill in the boxes.

	Amount	Description
Cost 1 £	1,200	Total
Cost 2 £		
Cost 3 £		
Cost 4 £		
Cost 5 £		
Cost 6 £		
Cost 7 £		
Cost 8 £		

The calculations

Contribution = Price − Variable Costs
$$= 1.00 - 0.5$$
$$= 0.5$$

$$\text{Breakeven Point} = \frac{\text{Fixed Costs}}{\text{Contributions}}$$

$$= \frac{1,200}{0.5}$$

$$= 2,400$$

Expected Profit = (Contribution × Expected Sales) − Fixed Costs
$$= (0.5 \times 5,000) - 1,200$$
$$= 1,300$$

Fig. 7.1   Business viability chart for case 1

busiest time. However, on average she spends £500 per week to generate a turnover of around £1,000. She never operates on less than 100 per cent margins and has learnt to be very sensitive to the need to change colours and styles to meet different fashions and seasons. She also limits cashflow problems by often buying on the Sunday with money taken on Saturday when business is good. As usual with market traders in a VAT-avoiding cash business, she says she knows her margins but only approximate turnover and hasn't a clue as to her profit. However, she thinks it could be a good idea to design and make clothes herself in the future and has found suitable premises near her flat, which she can buy for £30,000. However, she has no accounts, nor an accountant, and wants her bank manager to advise her whether the proposition makes sense, even though she is confident it is a winner.

Jane's business costs are as follows:

- Stall frames and covers: £200 per year
- Street market licence: £100 per year
- Staff: £20 per day
- Rent: £30 per Sunday, £12 per Saturday
- Music: £8 per week on tapes and batteries for her 'ghetto blaster'
- Bags: £3 per week for a turnover of £1,000
- Ironing: £5 per week on average
- Petrol: £5 per week on average

In addition to these costs Jane has a mortgage on her flat which, together with rates etc., comes to £320 per month. Historically her course grant had covered much of these costs but she is confident that her experience over three years in the market has made her sufficiently more efficient and profitable that she can cope now that the course, and grant, are coming to an end. She estimates that she spends approximately £100 per week on herself although, as she deals so much in cash, she doesn't really know. A bank loan paid for her car which costs, including interest payments, £3,000 per year. Her overdraft is less than £1,000.

Is Jane's business proposal viable? Do you think she is a winner?

Solution

There is no single product, price or unit costs, therefore, the breakeven analysis must be done in terms of sales revenue, based on a profit margin which is 100 per cent of her costs. Hence, only stages 2–6 of a breakeven analysis are needed.

- *Stage 2*: What are the variable costs?
  The major variable cost is the cost of her goods, which is 50p for every £1 of revenue.
  The only other variable cost is for the bags. Jane spends £3 for every £1,000 of sales so this cost is 0.3 per cent of turnover and, to keep the numbers simple, we will ignore it.
  Variable costs = £0.5 per £1 sales
- *Stage 3*: What is the contribution?
  Contribution = Price − Variable Costs
  $$= 1 - 0.5$$
  $$= 0.5$$
- *Stage 4*: What are the fixed costs?
  Her fixed costs per annum are:
  Stall frames: £200
  Licence: £100
  Staff: £2,080 (20 × 2 × 52)
  Rent: £2,184 (30 + 12 × 52)
  Music: £416 (8 × 52)
  Ironing: £260 (5 × 52)
  Petrol: £260 (5 × 52)
  Personal costs: £12,040 (320 × 12 + 100 × 52 + 3,000)
  Total: £17,540
- *Stage 5*: What is the breakeven point?
  $$\text{Breakeven Point} = \frac{\text{Fixed Costs}}{\text{Contribution}}$$
  $$= \frac{17,540}{0.5}$$
  $$= 35,080$$
  Jane needs a turnover of £35,080 to break even.
- *Stage 6*: What is the expected profit?
  This is the profit based on the best estimate of the sales volume.
  On sales of £50,000 Jane's profit is calculated:
  Profit = Volume × Contribution − Fixed Costs
  $$= 50,000 \times 0.5 - 17,540$$
  $$= £7,460$$

Whilst Jane's lack of cash and her stock of only £1,000 might tend to disprove her assertion that she spends only £100 per week on herself, it is quite clear that the business is viable. It would be more so if she made an additional 25 per cent mark-up by making some clothes herself, as well as missing out the wholesalers. In theory, she can certainly afford the £30,000 investment.

These breakeven calculations are shown in Jane's Business Viability Chart in Fig. 7.2.

46   Is the business viable?

Please fill in your answers to questions 1 to 6.

1   Do you want to work in terms of units sold or money? If you have one product
     you will probably choose units sold. If you have more than one product you
     will probably choose money.

     Please tick: Units sold [   ]
                    Money   [✓   ]

2A   **Answer this question only if you ticked units sold in question 1. If you
     ticked money go on to question 2B.**
     What is the selling price in £s?
          Please fill in the box.

     Price: £ [   ]

     What number of units do you expect to sell? (You can choose per week, per
     month or per year, but whatever time period you choose, you must keep to
     it for the rest of the analysis).
          Please fill in the box.

     Expected units sold: [   ]

     Now go to question 3.

2B   **Answer this question only if you ticked money in question 1.**
     What is you expected sales revenue, in £s? (You can choose per week, per
     month or per year, but whatever time period you choose, you must keep to
     it for the rest of the analysis).
          Please fill in the box.

     Expected Sales Revenue: £ [50,000]

     Now go to question 4.

3   What are the variable costs per item, in £s?
          Please fill in the boxes.

	Amount	Description
Cost 1 £		
Cost 2 £		
Cost 3 £		
Cost 4 £		
Cost 5 £		
Cost 6 £		
Cost 7 £		
Cost 8 £		

4   What are the costs which are percentage of price or sales revenue?
    Please fill in the boxes.

	Percentage		Description
Cost 1	0.3	%	Bags
Cost 2		%	
Cost 3		%	
Cost 4		%	

5   **Answer this question only if you ticked money in question 1. Otherwise go on to question 6.**
    Is there a cost in Profit Margin terms, e.g. when pricing is on a cost plus basis?

	Profit Margin		Description
	100	%	Mark-up

6   What are the fixed costs, in £s? Make sure each cost covers the same time period, e.g. weekly, monthly, yearly.
    Please fill in the boxes.

	Amount	Description
Cost 1 £	200	Stall frames
Cost 2 £	100	Licence
Cost 3 £	2,080	Staff
Cost 4 £	2,184	Rent
Cost 5 £	416	Music
Cost 6 £	260	Ironing
Cost 7 £	260	Petrol
Cost 8 £	12,040	Personal expenses

The calculations

Contribution = Price − Variable Costs
             = 1.00 − 0.5
             = 0.5

$$\text{Breakeven Point} = \frac{\text{Fixed Costs}}{\text{Contributions}}$$

$$= \frac{17,540}{0.5}$$

$$= 35,080$$

Expected Profit = (Contribution × Expected Sales) − Fixed Costs
                = (0.5 × 50,000) − 17,540
                = 25,000 − 17,540
                = 7,460

Fig. 7.2   Business viability chart for case 4

Comment

If the police and local government officials realised how vital London's street markets are to encouraging and fostering the growth of small businesses, they might be more helpful over petty infringements of trading and parking laws. In any event Jane's case demonstrates how it is possible to make serious money in a relatively short time on a purely part-time basis, invariably a very sensible way of 'testing the water' before taking the plunge. It also demonstrates that, in what is essentially the black economy, the reality of pound coins rather than till rolls and 'books' never helps you analyse whether you really have 'a nice little earner' or not. Jane herself is a very sophisticated 'Arthur Daley', but she hadn't a clue how much she had earned in her three years.

8 Handling more complex businesses

Theme: Breakeven analysis, although simple, can be applied to complex financial problems in small business

The next case illustrates a breakeven analysis concerned with the setting up of an exporting business.

Case 5: The exporter

Richard was a £12,000 a year export sales manager of a very small DIY company until it was bought out by a larger company. The new management was not interested in either exports or the new sealing product for which he had just finished negotiating distribution rights with sales agents in Scandinavia.

The redundancy deal eventually offered at Richard's suggestion was as follows:

- six months salary.
- European rights to market the sealing product.
- all related purchasing (1 year's supply) to be sold to Richard at cost when used, with no charges for design and tooling costs.
- his one year old company car (at book value – £4,000).

The agency deals that Richard had negotiated in four different countries were based on a guaranteed minimum annual purchase of 3,000 units per country which gave each agent exclusivity and their own design label and logo in the appropriate language. However, he had complete confidence that Denmark and Sweden would order at least twice this amount. Each unit would be sold at £2.15, 60 days C.I.F. Scandinavian port – hence Richard would have to pay for carriage from factory to the docks in the UK, insurance of the product until it reached the customer and sea freight, and would then have to wait 60 days for payment.

After further negotiations with a specialist contract packer, Richard determined that his direct manufacturing costs would be £1,000 per thousand units which would include free storage of the other packing materials until use and no charges on the packed stock until it was shipped. In addition, the contract packer gave Richard 90 days credit. He calculated that the other packaging costs were £100 per thousand, insurance would cost £15 and freight and carriage £100 per shipment of 3,000 units. Over and above these costs Richard calculated he would need to make, at best, one sales trip a year to Scandinavia at a cost of £1,000. Also, at a personal level, he calculated that, including running the car, his own personal expenditure would be around £750 per month which would also include his own limited office expenses.

However, having completed his research, Richard was phoned by one of his contacts and offered a similar job to his previous one at a similar salary. Should he take the risks of starting out on his own?

Solution

● *Stage 1*: What's the unit price of the product?
The sealing product is sold for £2.15.

● *Stage 2*: What are the variable costs?

Product: £1 $\left(\dfrac{£1,000}{1,000 \text{ units}}\right)$

Packaging: 10p $\left(\dfrac{£100}{1,000 \text{ units}}\right)$

Insurance: 0.5p $\left(\dfrac{£15}{3,000 \text{ units}}\right)$

Freight & Carriage: 3.33p $\left(\dfrac{£100}{3,000 \text{ units}}\right)$

Total: £1.14p to the nearest 1p.

● *Stage 3*: What is the contribution?

$$\begin{aligned}
\text{Contribution} &= \text{Price } - \text{ Variable Costs} \\
&= 2.15 - 1.14 \\
&= £1.01
\end{aligned}$$

● *Stage 4*: What are the fixed costs?
His fixed costs per annum are:
Car purchase: £4,000
Sales trip: £1,000
Personal expenses: £9,000 (12 × 750)

Car depreciation: £2,000 $\left(\dfrac{4,000}{2} : \begin{array}{l}\text{replacement by a similar} \\ \text{model in 2 years time}\end{array}\right)$

Total = £16,000

- *Stage 5*: What is the breakeven point?

$$\text{Breakeven point} = \frac{\text{Fixed Costs}}{\text{Contribution}}$$

$$= \frac{16,000}{1.01}$$

$$= 15,841 \text{ units}$$

- *Stage 6*: What is the expected profit?

  This is the profit based on the best estimate of the sales volume. Assuming that Richard's estimates are realistic, he should sell 18,000 units (4 countries × 3,000 units + 6,000 extra for Denmark and Sweden).

$$\begin{aligned}\text{Yearly Profit} &= \text{Volume} \times \text{Contribution} - \text{Fixed Costs}\\ &= 18,000 \times £1.01 - £16,000\\ &= £2,180\end{aligned}$$

These calculations are shown in Fig. 8.1.

Even if Richard is really confident about his sales forecast, this profit over and above his personal expenses of £9,000 (some of which he could offset against tax) would mean that he would be not much better off in his new venture, at least in year 1. Perhaps he could minimise his risk by negotiating a deal whereby he could do both jobs. This would be feasible since he is unlikely to be fully occupied with the sealing product alone, especially if in year 1 he wishes to limit his sales efforts to Scandinavia. In either event he can realistically say that the venture is probably worth the risk (given that his car purchase is a one-off addition to his fixed costs) and provided the cashflow difficulties he may have exporting to a very seasonal market like Scandinavia do not impose impossible problems.

Comment

In practice Richard, whilst rejecting the offer of another similar job, did get another part-time sales agency to help him make ends meet whilst establishing his own Scandinavian business. It was fortunate for him that he did. One year later his sales forecast had proved accurate only for Norway. The good news was that Sweden had taken 9,000 units but Finland had taken nothing (his Finnish agent was arrested by the Finnish tax authorities one day after signing the contract!). Critically, the Danish government had banned his product from Danish shops, despite it containing no substance disallowed by EC regulations. He had to pay to bring back the whole load. Moral: exporting can indeed be profitable but a small company which

Please fill in your answers to questions 1 to 6.

1   Do you want to work in terms of units sold or money? If you have one product
     you will probably choose units sold. If you have more than one product you
     will probably choose money.

     Please tick: Units sold | ✓ |
                    Money | |

2A   **Answer this question only if you ticked units sold in question 1. If you
     ticked money go on to question 2B.**
     What is the selling price in £s?
          Please fill in the box.

          Price: £ | 2.15 |

     What number of units do you expect to sell? (You can choose per week, per
     month or per year, but whatever time period you choose, you must keep to
     it for the rest of the analysis).
          Please fill in the box.

          Expected units sold: | 18,000 |

     Now go to question 3.

2B   **Answer this question only if you ticked money in question 1.**
     What is you expected sales revenue, in £s? (You can choose per week, per
     month or per year, but whatever time period you choose, you must keep to
     it for the rest of the analysis).
          Please fill in the box.

          Expected Sales Revenue: £ | |

     Now go to question 4.

3   What are the variable costs per item, in £s?
          Please fill in the boxes.

	Amount	Description
Cost 1 £	1.00	Product
Cost 2 £	0.10	Packaging
Cost 3 £	0.005	Insurance
Cost 4 £	0.033	Freight
Cost 5 £		
Cost 6 £		
Cost 7 £		
Cost 8 £		

4   What are the costs which are percentage of price or sales revenue?
     Please fill in the boxes.

	Percentage	Description
Cost 1	%	
Cost 2	%	
Cost 3	%	
Cost 4	%	

5   **Answer this question only if you ticked money in question 1. Otherwise
     go on to question 6.**
     Is there a cost in Profit Margin terms, e.g. when pricing is on a cost plus basis?

	Profit Margin	Description
	%	

6   What are the fixed costs, in £s? Make sure each cost covers the same time
     period, e.g. weekly, monthly, yearly.
     Please fill in the boxes.

	Amount	Description
Cost 1 £	4,000	Car purchase
Cost 2 £	1,000	Sales trip
Cost 3 £	9,000	Personal expenses
Cost 4 £	2,000	Car depreciation
Cost 5 £		
Cost 6 £		
Cost 7 £		
Cost 8 £		

The calculations

$$\text{Contribution} = \text{Price} - \text{Variable Costs}$$
$$= 2.15 - 1.14$$
$$= 1.01$$

$$\text{Breakeven Point} = \frac{\text{Fixed Costs}}{\text{Contributions}}$$
$$= \frac{16,000}{1.01}$$
$$= 15,841$$

$$\text{Expected Profit} = (\text{Contribution} \times \text{Expected Sales}) - \text{Fixed Costs}$$
$$= (1.01 \times 18,000) - 16,000$$
$$= 2,180$$

Fig. 8.1   Business viability chart for case 5

bases success solely on exports, without having a secure home market, is forever hostage to fortune in one form or another; whether it be an ultra-green Danish government, a dock strike or a British Chancellor building a strong pound and thus preventing price rises.

Case 6: The bookshop

In 1985 Allan West, together with a partner, purchased a long established bookshop in London's West End. Whilst the bookshop had a turnover of some £500,000 its overheads had for some time ensured that it had traded only at breakeven level. This was why they had had the opportunity to buy a long established bookshop for just £60,000. They had raised the money from the bank, together with their working capital requirements, by a loan of £25,000 and by giving the bank a charge of £25,000 on each of their houses and a personal guarantee of £10,000.

By 1988 turnover had been increased substantially, but so had overheads, despite Allan's partner taking another job to keep the two directors' salary costs down to a low level (£30,000, divided equally). Allan's solution was to recommend a growth strategy involving re-decorating, computerisation for better stock control and shelf utilisation, and sustained effort to expand sales to their blue chip major customers. Allan's partner disagreed to the point where he recommended selling the bookshop lease and establishing a basically wholesale operation to those major customers from the equivalent of a small factory unit.

The differences were fundamental and irrevocable. Allan resolved to buy out his partner and press on with his strategy. His partner was not unwilling to sell at a price which naturally included his release from their joint guarantees to the bank. There was, therefore, only the one further hurdle – the £60,000 of additional cash, security and guarantees Allan had to pay his partner and give to the bank. However, he had only just completed paying for his children's education by way of a 'top up' mortgage. He didn't have either the £25,000 cash or the collateral that the bank would accept as suitable security for a £25,000 loan and £35,000 additional guarantees over and above what he had already given. After some consideration he was able to offer his bank security for an additional £40,000 by handing over a family trust fund and insurance policy. Unfortunately the bank manager would not budge an inch, despite agreeing with Allan's overall growth strategy.

At this stage Allan realised he needed help in the form of some professional and objective appraisal of whether he should battle on in his efforts to get rid of his partner – or even if his strategy was right in the first place. His first reaction was to see his accountant but he rejected this option as he was unhappy with his obvious lack of 'hands on' small business experience. Somewhat as an afterthought he rang up Paul, one of his old lecturers on a business school small business course he had attended some years previously when he had originally decided to shift from a major multi-national into small business. Paul's subsequent visit to the well-situated but dreadfully laid-out and decorated shop and his analysis of the management accounts led to Paul accepting Allan's offer of a non-executive directorship, at a fee of £5,000 per year, and a joint declaration that the strategy was broadly correct and that Allan's original plan should, therefore, proceed.

These were the salient points of the management accounts from the previous year:

Sales	600	(includes Dec. peak and July/Aug. trough)
Stock	60	
Cost of goods sold	450	
Other variable costs	18	
Fixed costs	130	(includes all wage and salary costs)
Overdraft	50	
Bank charges	5	
Loss	3	

NB 1. All figures in thousands
    2. Ignore VAT consideration
    3. Assume 30 days creditors and debtors except December which is 75 per cent cash receipts.

What had Paul seen in the overall picture that Allan's bank manager hadn't and how would that be of use in Allan's search for the £60,000?

What Paul was able to analyse was that whilst the existence of the Net Book Agreement (fixed prices and margins for booksellers) made the improvement of trading margins and hence profitability extremely difficult, the effect of the departure of Allan's partner on the profitability of the company was much more marked. From the case we know that Allan's partner costs a minimum of £15,000 (in practice he would cost more by virtue of his use of phones, insurances, etc.). He already works infrequently at the shop so no direct replacement costs are necessary. Paul, however, will cost an extra £5,000. The effects on profitability are to lower fixed costs by £10,000 and thereby increasing profits by the same amount. As the cost of buying out the partner is £25,000, a loan over, for example, five years for that amount at 15 per cent interest rates could be calculated simply as costing the following:

Year 1 8,750 (5,000 repaid + interest on 25,000)
Year 2 8,000 (5,000 repaid + interest on 20,000)
Year 3 7,250 (5,000 repaid + interest on 15,000)
Year 4 6,500 (5,000 repaid + interest on 10,000)
Year 5 5,750 (5,000 repaid + interest on 5,000)

Consequently Paul realised that, even in Year 1, getting rid of Allan's partner saved the company £1,250 (i.e. £15,000 salary − £5,000 (Paul's fee) − £8,750 loan costs). Moreover, it made the bank's investment *less* risky by virtue of solving the constant disputes between 50/50 partners which, if they had reached total breakdown and non-agreement, would have ended with the business having to be sold in order for the partners to go their separate ways. Hence, he argued, the present bank manager was being remarkably short-sighted even in strictly financial terms. This, coupled with the bank manager's acceptance of Allan's strategy to expand sales, made his refusal to help the buy-out inexplicable.

Paul therefore introduced Allan to his local NatWest manager who looked at several years' figures (roughly on a par with those given). He also came down to the West End, spent time with Allan getting a feel for the place and several hours chatting to Allan and Paul about their strategy over the next four years. The result was an offer to Allan on terms which included the key phrase, 'I will accept a £20,000 commercial risk on behalf of the bank to bridge the gap between what you need and what collateral you can offer'.

Solution

Whilst the accounts give a loss position of £3,000, it is always sensible to check this using breakeven analysis. The calculations are shown in Fig. 8.2. The breakeven point is a turnover of £591,000.

The moral of this story is that all sets of accounts are capable of some adjustment. Here Allan has not included bank charges as a fixed cost. Try the calculations again:

$$\text{Breakeven} = \frac{\text{Fixed Costs}}{\text{Contribution}}$$

$$= \frac{135}{0.22}$$

$$= £613.6$$

As he has actually sold £600,000 his yearly profit/loss is:

$$\begin{aligned}
\text{Yearly Profit} &= \text{Volume} \times \text{Contribution} - \text{Fixed Costs} \\
&= 600 \times 0.22 - 135 \\
&= -3
\end{aligned}$$

So our calculations agree with Allan's; he is indeed making a very small loss. However, it's of more use to ask what the effect on profitability would be if Allan could increase sales by 10 per cent:

$$\begin{aligned}
\text{Yearly Profit} &= \text{Volume} \times \text{Contribution} - \text{Fixed Costs} \\
&= 660 \times 0.22 - 135 \\
&= 10.2 \\
&= \text{Happiness (relatively!)}
\end{aligned}$$

In any event, Allan and Paul now know that to make a small profit next year they need to sell roughly £50,000 worth more books, whilst keeping overheads the same.

Comment

The real point of this case is how very lucky Allan was to be able to part reasonably amicably from his 50/50 partner. Normally this very common situation is as disastrous as failed marriages when 'love' turns to 'hate'; logic, objectivity and commonsense fly straight out of the window. So please remember that 50/50 partnerships are invariably fraught with risk. If you still insist in getting into one, at least get your solicitor to draw up a *management* agreement as well as a *partnership* agreement, spelling out who will have overall authority in a dispute and how the assets will be sorted out in the event of a 'divorce'.

Another point to be noticed is that neither bank manager was prepared to lend any money to the business on the basis of the £60,000 stock, despite its self-evident saleability. When bank managers do lend against stock they usually take a very conservative estimate of its value. In this case, the problem in determining whether

58 Is the business viable?

Please fill in your answers to questions 1 to 6.

1   Do you want to work in terms of units sold or money? If you have one product you will probably choose units sold. If you have more than one product you will probably choose money.

Please tick: Units sold

Units sold	
Money	✓

2A   **Answer this question only if you ticked units sold in question 1. If you ticked money go on to question 2B.**
What is the selling price in £s?
     Please fill in the box.

Price: £ [   ]

What number of units do you expect to sell? (You can choose per week, per month or per year, but whatever time period you choose, you must keep to it for the rest of the analysis).
     Please fill in the box.

Expected units sold: [   ]

Now go to question 3.

2B   **Answer this question only if you ticked money in question 1.**
What is you expected sales revenue, in £s? (You can choose per week, per month or per year, but whatever time period you choose, you must keep to it for the rest of the analysis).
     Please fill in the box.

Expected Sales Revenue: £ [*600,000*]

Now go to question 4.

3   What are the variable costs per item, in £s?
     Please fill in the boxes.

	Amount	Description
Cost 1 £		
Cost 2 £		
Cost 3 £		
Cost 4 £		
Cost 5 £		
Cost 6 £		
Cost 7 £		
Cost 8 £		

4   What are the costs which are percentage of price or sales revenue?
     Please fill in the boxes.

	Percentage	Description
Cost 1	%	
Cost 2	%	
Cost 3	%	
Cost 4	%	

5 **Answer this question only if you ticked money in question 1. Otherwise go on to question 6.**
Is there a cost in Profit Margin terms, e.g. when pricing is on a cost plus basis?

Profit Margin	Description
28.2 %	Cost of goods sold + other variable costs

6 What are the fixed costs, in £s? Make sure each cost covers the same time period, e.g. weekly, monthly, yearly.
    Please fill in the boxes.

	Amount	Description
Cost 1 £	130,000	Total
Cost 2 £		
Cost 3 £		
Cost 4 £		
Cost 5 £		
Cost 6 £		
Cost 7 £		
Cost 8 £		

The calculations
Pre-Calculations:

$$\frac{\text{Variable Costs}}{\text{Sales}} = \frac{468}{600}$$
$$= 0.78$$

Contribution = Price − Variable Costs
$$= 1.00 - 0.78$$
$$= 0.22$$

$$\text{Breakeven Point} = \frac{\text{Fixed Costs}}{\text{Contributions}}$$

$$= \frac{130}{0.22}$$

$$= 591$$

Expected Profit = (Contribution × Expected Sales) − Fixed Costs

Fig. 8.2 Business viability chart for case 6

the stock was indeed saleable stock or really 'glossy remainders', coupled with its potential for instant removal, before the bank could repossess it if necessary, made the prospect a non-starter. The result was the strange irony of a bank manager lending £20,000 with no security rather than against £60,000 of stock. A further irony in this case was that the original bank manager involved was most upset when he lost the account!

The numerical information for this case was worked out entirely on a Business Viability Chart which is all you need to do almost any breakeven analysis. A blank BVC is at the back of the book for you to investigate your own businesses or business ideas.

9   Survivability

Theme: Will there be sufficient cash?

The name Rolls Royce should be forever in every small business person's mind because, when Rolls Royce went spectacularly bust in 1973 and had to be rescued by the government, it was actually trading *profitably*. It had just run out of cash (i.e. it had come against its borrowing limits) and the banks were not prepared to lend more. If it can happen to Rolls Royce, it can happen a lot more easily to a small business.

Problems are often caused by the natural unevenness of payments both incoming and outgoing and the unpredictability of some of these payments, usually critical incoming payments, being made on time. At the lowest level it might be a strike at a DHSS office stopping your Enterprise Allowance. More often it is a big customer taking that extra two weeks' credit; in any event the effect can be serious, particularly if you have little room for financial manoeuvre and even more so if you have not kept your bank manager informed. It matters little what the reasons are, bank managers are *always* less than impressed by small business customers explaining problems *after* they have gone over agreed overdraft limits. The solution is a little planning and some simple management information.

Before we tackle this however, let us firstly 'lay some ghosts' about cashflows. Consider the following two documents:

- a NatWest current issue *Cashflow Forecast* (see Fig. 9.1)
- our extremely simple offering also labelled 'Cashflow Forecast' (see Fig. 9.2)

To a trained banker or accountant our cashflow forecast is far too simplistic. It is better than nothing, but of limited use to him. He will find his much more detailed chart with all its different headings infinitely more revealing. On the other hand, to a small business person our simple chart is about as much as he or she can cope with before 'numbers switch-off' occurs. Significantly, both documents fulfil exactly the same purpose; the difference is that only one party – the banker – understands both instantly. In fact, the

	Enter Month											
	Figures rounded to **£ 's**	Budget	Actual	Budget	Actual	Budget	Actual	Budget	Actual	Budget	Actual	Bu
	Receipts											
1	Sales (inc VAT) – Cash											
2	– Debtors											
3	Other Trading Income											
4	Loans Received											
5	Capital Introduced											
6	Disposal of Assets											
7	Other Receipts											
A	**Total Receipts**											
	Payments											
8	Cash Purchases											
9	Payments to Creditors											
10	Principals Remuneration											
11	Wages/Salaries (net)											
12	PAYE/NI											
13	Capital Items											
14	Transport/Packaging											
15	Rent/Rates											
16	Services											
17	Loan Repayments											
18	HP/Leasing Repayments											
19	Interest											
20	Bank/Finance Charges											
21	Professional Fees											
22	Advertising											
23												
24												
25												
26	VAT											
27	Corporation Tax etc											
28	Dividends											
B	**Total Payments**											
C	**Net Cashflow (A – B)**											
29	Opening Bank Balance											
D	**Closing Bank** **Balance (C ± Line 29)**											

Basic Assumptions – Please specify the following assumptions used in completing this form and list any other relevant ones ove
– Credit Taken   – the average period taken from creditors.   _____ Days
– Credit Given   – the average period given to debtors.   _____ Days

Fig. 9.1   Cashflow forecast

	Budget	Actual	Budget	Actual	Budget	Actual	Budget	Actual	Budget	Actual	Budget	Actual	Total Budget	Total Actual
ual														

Cash Forecast

	JAN	FEB	MAR	APR	MAY	JUN	JUL	AUG	SEP	OCT	NOV	DEC
SALES												
VARIABLE COSTS (usually purchases)												
FIXED COSTS (usually overheads)												
SALARY												
NET CASH (Sales less expenses)												
OVERDRAFT REQUIREMENTS												

Fig. 9.2   Cashflow forecast

NatWest form is relatively straightforward compared to any bank's letter of credit form.

Most banks' cashflow or budget charts are very useful as checklists to make sure all items of expense and income are included. In practice you should fill them in, because banks insist that you do, but you may then *ignore* them if you want to. Instead, we say you should produce the half a dozen or so *key* numbers – critical measures of your performance – which are contained in our chart. They must be produced, and understood, and you ignore them at your *greatest peril*.

If you are losing money by the bucketful, or about to start to, our chart will demonstrate it clearly. You should concentrate on this bare minimum of numerical information until your confidence and competence build and you can handle more and more. This should start to happen as you work through each case in turn.

Case 1: The Fish and Chip shop

Let us first look at the Fish and Chip shop case-study to illustrate the basics of cashflow forecasting. Before proceeding you may like to remind yourself of the facts of the case.

From the information, we know that Harry's sales forecast is 5,000 portions sold each month at £1 per portion. Hence 5,000 can be entered on the cashflow forecast chart (Fig. 9.3) in each month in the sales row. We also know from the case study that Harry expects each portion to cost him just over 49p. So, keeping the mathematics simple, Harry can enter £2,500 along the variable cost row (5,000 portions × 50p). The fixed costs of £1,200 per month given in the case study included the money Harry pays himself for living expenses. Since salary is such an important element of costs, it is separated from other fixed costs in the cashflow chart. Assuming Harry only pays himself £100 per week initially (£400 per month), the fixed costs row can be filled in with £800 per month (£1,200 less the £400 Harry is going to pay himself) and the salary row with the remaining £400 per month. You can assume reasonably that Harry will be living in the flat above the shop and hence has no other personal costs being paid on a regular basis.

These figures enable Harry to work out that in his first month's trading (assuming that suppliers will give him a normal one month's credit and that he does not have to pay more than £800 fixed costs) he will not need an overdraft facility and that he should have £1,300 in the bank.

9

Cash Forecast

	JAN	FEB	MAR	APR	MAY	JUN	JUL	AUG	SEP	OCT	NOV	DEC
SALES	5000	5000	5000	5000	5000	5000	5000	5000	5000	5000	5000	5000
VARIABLE COSTS (usually purchases)	2500	2500	2500	2500	2500	2500	2500	2500	2500	2500	2500	2500
FIXED COSTS (usually overheads)	800	800	800	800	800	800	800	800	800	800	800	800
SALARY	400	400	400	400	400	400	400	400	400	400	400	400
NET CASH (Sales less expenses)	1300	2600	3900	5200	6500	7800	9100	10,400	11,700	13,000	14,300	15,600
OVERDRAFT REQUIREMENTS	N/A	N/A	N/A	N/A	N/A	N/A	N/A	N/A	N/A	N/A	N/A	N/A

Fig. 9.3 Cash flow chart for case 1

Net cash = Sales
        − Variable costs
        − Fixed costs
        − Salary
   = 5,000 − 2,500 − 800 − 400
   = £1,300

If everything goes to forecast, Harry will have over £15,000 in the bank by the end of the year. Things may not work out quite so well, but if Harry compares his *actual* expenditure with his *forecast* each month, he will at least know where the problems are and what to do about them.

In practice, of course, business life is never as smooth as the example of Harry's Fish and Chip shop. Sales vary and are on credit terms unlike Harry's fish and chips which is an all-cash sales business. Fish and potatoes are perishable and easily replaced at very short notice, therefore, not much stock is held and what is can easily be measured. This is by no means true of many businesses where much more guesswork has to be used when estimating sales and stock levels.

Similarly, fixed costs are *never* in real life totally constant from month to month by virtue of phone bills, bank charges, gas, electricity and VAT bills all arriving every three months. Equally, with the best will in the world, most people cannot forecast their personal expenditure every month. Holidays, vehicle breakdowns, school bills and Christmas are just some of the reasons why fluctuations occur.

However, the principles of this simplistic approach hold good for all businesses and you must try and make the most accurate forecast possible before you start in business and then, without exception, compare actual results with forecasts each month. The other major problem in practice is that cashflows are often delayed, for example goods sold in March may be made from materials bought in January and February, and not paid for until June. VAT can also cause problems of this type. In general, when making your own cash-flow forecast, always include the cashflow only *when it occurs:* a sale is not a sale until it is *paid for*.

Comment

The figures in this case may well make appealing reading to would-be shop owners. However, always remember the downside. For example:

9

1. Cash businesses are a double-edged sword. When it is the proprietor's hand in the till, it is his or her business, literally. But the fast food chains have found out the hard way that even sophisticated electronics can't stop 'leakage', as staff theft is so euphemistically known. Hence, unless Harry is very very lucky he will need to be there every day, if not every hour the shop is open at least until he gets to know his staff intimately.

2. Fish and Chip shops or equivalent are open on just the times guaranteed to wreck any concept of normal social life. So if you like a drink on Friday and Saturday night, forget it. And on the subject of Harry's social life we hope his girlfriend is very tolerant or has lost her sense of smell – that fish and chip smell really does get everywhere.

3. If you are thinking of opening a shop in your 'nice little town' with that redundancy cheque or inheritance money because there isn't a boutique, cheese shop, golf shop or whatever in town – then stop and think. First, always remember that very few people travel to a small business: restaurants are one of the few exceptions. So, if the total population is, for example, 30,000 and you need 500 people spending £1 per week to break even, forget it. Not convinced? Try a simple calculation like this:

30,000 divided by 4 (to calculate number of families)
7,500 divided by 2 (to adjust for children)
3,750 divided by 52 (weeks of the year)

Answer: a maximum of only 72 potential customers per week, assuming each customer makes one purchase per year.

10 Survivability: the case studies

Theme: More examples of cashflow analysis?

The case of Harry's Fish and Chip shop helped us to look at the ideas behind a simple cashflow analysis but it did not present any real practical problems. We now take up the other five case studies we have investigated so far and see what cashflow problems they have. In returning to the cases we will pick a range of issues related to cashflow such as seasonal trading, factoring and the purchase of capital assets.

In Harry's case the price of buying the shop was not reflected in the cashflow. However, purchasing a car does present a cashflow problem for David's driving instruction business.

Case 2: The driving instructor

Before proceeding you may like to remind yourself of the facts of the case (see Fig. 10.1).

David's sales forecast is £975 per month (£7.50 per lesson × 30 hours × 52 weeks i.e. 12 months). This assumes that factors such as holidays, sickness and weather, which would reduce the £975, can be compensated for by David working longer hours. David's variable costs are entirely related to running the car and whilst service bills are not constant they are not likely to throw out the figures too much if an average cost of £260 per month is used (10p per mile × 20 miles per lesson × 30 lessons per week × 52 weeks per year i.e. 12 months).

The first fixed cost is the interest on the loan which David used to buy his car. Assuming that a car finance company would lend him £9,500, at a flat rate of 10 per cent per annum repaid over a two-year period, David will have to pay £475 per month (£9,500 + £1,900 interest divided by 24). In addition, he will have to pay £173 per month advertising (40 × 52 − 12) and £173 per month for administrative costs.

Depreciation is not a cash amount. Although the viability analysis allowed £80 per week for the decreasing value of his car, David

Cash Forecast

	JAN	FEB	MAR	APR	MAY	JUN	JUL	AUG	SEP	OCT	NOV	DEC
SALES	975	975	975	975	975	975	975	975	975	975	975	975
VARIABLE COSTS (usually purchases)	260	260	260	260	260	260	260	260	260	260	260	260
FIXED COSTS (usually overheads)	821	821	821	821	821	821	821	821	821	821	821	821
SALARY	200	200	200	200	200	200	200	200	200	200	200	200
NET CASH (Sales less expenses)	(306)*	(612)	(918)	(1224)	(1530)	(1836)	(2142)	(2448)	(2754)	(3060)	(3366)	(3672)
OVERDRAFT REQUIREMENTS												

* The brackets indicate a minus sign

Fig. 10.1 Cashflow chart for case 2

does not actually pay £80 per week. The payment would be in a lump sum in two years' time when the car has to be replaced and this amount would be shown if the cashflow forecast covered a longer period. Depreciation is, therefore, not shown in cash statements which only record amounts actually paid.

David's total fixed costs are, therefore, £821 per month (475 + 173 + 173). Entering this figure and a minimal £200 for personal salary it can easily be seen that his cash position deteriorates even without allowing for the need to replace the car. A cash deficit of £3,670 at the end of the first year's trading is not necessarily a serious problem, but in this case David's ability to expand sales or cut costs is strictly limited. The cashflow forecast confirms the viability analysis. He should not proceed with this idea.

Comment

The saying that 'if you invent a better mousetrap the world will beat a path to your door' may be a truism but it happens very rarely indeed in the world of small business – no matter how marvellous your product. However, if David's total ambition lies in being a driving instructor even if it won't make him rich, then he must face the fact that in effect the cost of his dream is likely to be well over £10,000 before he is sufficiently well-known to 'sell' the 40+ lessons per week he needs to break even and pay himself even a small salary. Some people are addicted to their idea to such an extent that they will make this sort of sacrifice. Commendable perhaps, but don't expect any investor to agree – least of all a sensible bank manager.

Case 3: The antique dealer

10

Before proceeding you may like to remind yourself of the facts of this case (see Fig. 10.2).

The cashflow forecast in this case is complicated because the sales figures have to be different in the two halves of the year, reflecting the different stock levels. In the first six months, the stock level was £5,000 giving *annual* sales of £15,000. In the second six months, the stock level was £10,000 giving *annual* sales of £30,000. Consequently, sales figures of £1,250 per month (£7,500 divided by 6 months) and £2,500 (£15,000 divided by 6 months) can be inserted.

The variable costs are entirely purchases and it is known from the case that with profit margins of 35 per cent on cost, each £135

Cash Forecast	JAN	FEB	MAR	APR	MAY	JUN	JUL	AUG	SEP	OCT	NOV	DEC
SALES	1250	1250	1250	1250	1250	1250	2500	2500	2500	2500	2500	2500
VARIABLE COSTS (usually purchases)	925	925	925	925	925	925	1850	1850	1850	1850	1850	1850
FIXED COSTS (usually overheads)	650	650	650	650	650	650	650	650	650	650	650	650
SALARY	400	400	400	400	400	400	400	400	400	400	400	400
NET CASH (Sales less expenses)	(725)*	(1450)	(2175)	(2900)	(3625)	(4350)	(4750)	(5150)	(5550)	(5950)	(6350)	(6750)
OVERDRAFT LIMITS	5000	5000	5000	5000	5000	5000	10,000	10,000	10,000	10,000	10,000	10,000

* The brackets indicate a minus sign

Fig. 10.2 Cashflow chart for case 3

of sales has cost £100. For the first six months the variable costs are, therefore, £925 per month (100 ÷ 135 × £1,250) and £1,850 (100 ÷ 135 × £2,500) for the second six-month period.

There are two fixed costs – the hire of space of £2,600 (50 × 52 weeks) and the proportion of the £10,000 hiring costs which comprises the suitable car and its running costs. Let us assume that figure is £5,200, with £4,800 purely salary. This enables the fixed costs column to be completed (2,600 + 5,200 ÷ 12 months = 650).

On sales of £1,250 per month, John and Judy are losing money at the rate of £725 per month. When their sales rise to £2,500 per month, the loss is only reduced to £400. In consequence, by the end of the year, they will have lost £6,570 and still not have paid interest on the money borrowed from the bank to purchase stock or put any money aside to pay depreciation on their vehicle. Again, the cashflow confirms the breakeven analysis: without further funds to provide more stock the business must fail *given this sort of margin*.

Comment

This case illustrates clearly how large an amount of money has to be invested in stock for even a very small retail operation when the stock turn is only average. It also shows how rapidly cashflow (or lack of it) becomes a real problem in the event of a credit squeeze or interest rate hike depressing retail spending on such non-essentials as antiques, new kitchens and foreign holidays. It is, for example, difficult to have less than £20,000 stock in a 1,500 square feet shop.

This case also demonstrates how vicious life as a small business person can be. In practice John and Judy were unable to reconcile themselves to living with a £20,000 overdraft hanging over their heads, which was probably the minimum needed. They are no longer in the business.

Case 4: The market trader

The fourth case study, the market trader, introduces the problem of seasonality. In simple cashflow terms, there is no point in looking forward to fat months if you ran out of cash and went bust in the previous lean months. Jane demonstrates this problem very well having virtually no sales in January, February and March and not much more in April, but being very busy from September to Christmas. Hence the sales figures in the cashflow chart range from

£500 per month in the first three months of the year to £7,000 in the last four months (see Fig. 10.3).

Using the 100 per cent margin given in the case and ignoring the purchase of bags to keep the mathematics simple, it is then easy to fill in the variable cost row at exactly half the sales figures (500 sales − 250 cost of sales = 100 per cent margins).

Jane's fixed costs are more complicated but, as she works from home, it is probably best to include her mortgage as well as her car in fixed costs together with the other business costs listed in the case and these add up to £1,010 per month. The £420 in the salary column is the £100 which she pays herself rounded up slightly. As can be seen, whilst the business generates nearly £8,000 profit in the year, if she does not secure an overdraft of £4,500 in March and April she could be in trouble as her current personal overdraft of less than £1,000 does not indicate lots of savings to tide her over the lean months.

Comment

Jane's successful existence in the grey/black economy is of no use to her if her bank manager doesn't believe her oral figures. Would you? In practice, weather alone can make her sales even more variable without even considering the vagaries of the exchange rates (tourists or no tourists), mortgage rates (high rates always depress the sales of this type of product which by its nature is not essential) and, even more extreme, the closure of markets for 'redevelopment'. Equally Jane and many like her never get that £4,500 overdraft because, curiously, they've never asked for one. After all when you keep no figures how do you know you need one? Hence the credit card balances go haywire, the rent cheque gets delayed and a few hundred pounds are borrowed and she gets by, until next time. It is always worth remembering that bank managers are somewhat like priests: they do keep confidences and they don't work for the Inland Revenue. More importantly both like honesty and full confession of previous sins before helping to wipe the slate clean.

Case 5: The exporter

The fifth case study extends the problem of seasonality seen in Case 4 to include *credit* periods. It is, therefore, more complicated (see Fig. 10.4).

Cash Forecast

	JAN	FEB	MAR	APR	MAY	JUN	JUL	AUG	SEP	OCT	NOV	DEC
SALES	500	500	500	1500	4000	5000	5000	5000	7000	7000	7000	7000
VARIABLE COSTS (usually purchases)	250	250	250	750	2000	2500	2500	2500	3500	3500	3500	3500
FIXED COSTS (usually overheads)	1010	1010	1010	1010	1010	1010	1010	1010	1010	1010	1010	1010
SALARY	420	420	420	420	420	420	420	420	420	420	420	420
NET CASH (Sales less expenses)	(1180)*	(2360)	(3540)	(4220)	(3650)	(2580)	(1510)	(440)	1630	3700	5770	7840
OVERDRAFT REQUIREMENTS	1500	2500	4000	4500	4000	3000	2000	500	–	–	–	–

* The brackets indicate a minus sign

Fig. 10.3 Cashflow chart for case 4

10

Cash Forecast

		JAN	FEB	MAR	APR	MAY	JUN	JUL	AUG	SEP	OCT	NOV	DEC
SALES	Despatches (units)												
	Receipts (£s)	–	–	6000	3000	–	12,900	6450	3000	6000	–	6450	12,900
VARIABLE COSTS (usually purchases)	Product (£1 per unit)						6000	3000				3000	6000
	Packaging 14p Insurance } per Car, Freight } unit			840	420				420	840			
FIXED COSTS (usually overheads)	Car purchase + (sales trip)	4000					1000						
	SALARY	750	750	750	750	750	750	750	750	750	750	750	750
NET CASH (cumulative) (Sales less expenses)		(4750)*	(5500)	(7090)	(8260)	(9010)	(3860)	(1160)	(2330)	(3920)	(4676)	(1976)	4180
OVERDRAFT REQUIREMENTS		5000	5750	7250	8500	9250	4000	1250	2500	4000	4750	2000	–

Fig. 10.4   Cashflow chart for case 5

* The brackets indicate a minus sign

Scandinavia is a difficult market because of size (it is small and fragmented into four different countries) and because Norway, Finland and to a lesser degree Sweden, are frozen up for six months of the year, making DIY work impractical for that period. Therefore, it is reasonable that despatches will only take place in the Spring and Summer. Richard is expecting to sell 3,000 units per annum to Norway and Finland and 6,000 to Denmark and Sweden. It is reasonable to assume that he will, therefore, ship half the Danish and Swedish order in March and September and half the Norwegian and Finnish order in April and August. However, as he is giving 60 days' credit to his agents, he is unlikely to be paid until the third month after despatch (i.e. allowing 75 days in practice). Therefore, Denmark and Sweden's money will not be received until June when, assuming a January start, he has been in business for six months.

The cashflow position is worsened by his need to pay £4,000 for his ex-company car and the fact that packaging, insurance and transport costs will have to be, in all likelihood, paid in the same month as the goods are despatched. These costs must, therefore, be added to the £750 per month personal costs he will have incurred. However, the 90 days' credit which he receives from his packer will at least mean that he should not be too stretched and that his *main* bills will be paid in the month when he is paid.

Even by delaying his sales trip to June, his cashflow requirements will need overdraft facilities of over £9,000 (plus interest, in practice). Even if he lends his own six months' redundancy pay (£6,000 tax free) to his new business, he will still need significant support from his bank manager until December at the earliest and then again from March to June the next year.

10

Comment

Most bank managers given both Richard's experience and firm annual contracts from a 'safe' export market like Scandinavia are likely to be helpful. However, most are likely to demand some changes in Richard's plans so as to reduce *their* exposure. Firstly, they may well recommend a re-financing of the car so that Richard realises say £2 – 3,000 of the £4,000 purchase and lease-purchases the car over two years. This will reduce his capital outlay and overdraft requirement, albeit whilst increasing his variable costs by the price of a monthly lease.

Another suggestion from the bank could well be to factor the debts. This is by no means unfeasible for the Scandinavian market, with or without Export Credit Guarantees available for exporters. Moreover, the bank will require additional collateral. This might be a personal guarantee or second charge against his property. In practice Richard converted his £6,000 of redundancy money into Premium Bonds and left the certificates with the bank as cast-iron security for £6,000. As he was intending anyway to keep this as a nest-egg, using the Premium Bond route enabled him to avoid either personal guarantees or second charges and still have a chance of winning some prizes (actually, he won 13 × £50 in Year 1 and 5 × £50 in Year 2 — overall not a bad *tax-free* return).

Case 6: The bookshop

To recap on the original case, the management accounts were given as follows:

Sales	600	(includes a Dec. peak and July/Aug. trough)
Stock	60	
Cost of goods sold	450	
Variable costs	18	
Fixed costs	130	(includes all wage and salary costs)
Overdraft	50	
Bank charges	5	
Loss	3	

NB 1. All figures in thousands
2. Ignore VAT consideration
3. Assume 30 days creditors and debtors except December which is 75 per cent cash receipts.

We are also given that the two directors' salary is £30,000 split equally. So, with some reasonable assumptions, it is not difficult to fill in the cashflow chart (see Fig. 10.5).

Sales are given as £600,000 with a peak in December and a summer trough. This can be transcribed as £50,000 per month except December which has £100,000 and July/August which has £25,000. Similarly sales receipts are one month behind *actual* sales except December and January which show the effect of December's sales being 75 per cent cash.

Cash Forecast

All figures in '000s	JAN	FEB	MAR	APR	MAY	JUN	JUL	AUG	SEP	OCT	NOV	DEC	TOTAL
SALES													
Sales Receipts	50	50	50	50	50	50	25	25	50	50	50	100	600
	25	50	50	50	50	50	50	25	25	50	50	125	600
VARIABLE COSTS (usually purchases)	76.5	39	39	39	39	39	39	20.25	20.25	39	39	39	468
FIXED COSTS (usually overheads)	8.75	8.75	8.75	8.75	8.75	8.75	8.75	8.75	8.75	8.75	8.75	8.75	105
DIRECTORS' SALARY	2.5	2.5	2.5	2.5	2.5	2.5	2.5	2.5	2.5	2.5	2.5	2.5	30
NET CASH (cumulative) (sales less expenses)	(62.75)*	(63)	(63.25)	(63.5)	(63.75)	(64)	(64.25)	(70.75)	(77.75)	(78)	(3.5)	(3.5)	(5)
OVERDRAFT REQUIREMENTS	65	65	65	65	65	65	65	70	80	80	80	80	

* The brackets indicate a minus sign

Fig. 10.5   Cashflow chart for case 6

10

There are two variable costs:

- Cost of goods sold = 75 per cent of sales
  (Accounts show £600,000 sales and £450,000 cost of goods sold)
  To allow for credit this is based on the previous month's sales.
- Other variable costs = £1,500 per month
  (Accounts show £18,000 for the year)

Fixed costs are given in this case as £135,000 (fixed costs + bank charges) but for the cashflow chart we can use £105,000 (135,000 less directors' salary of 30,000). Meanwhile, since in practice bank charges and rent are spread throughout the year, it is not unreasonable to say that all these costs are unlikely to fall at the same time and so the cashflow chart can be filled in on the basis of £8,750 per month (105,000 ÷ 12). The salary column can be filled in at £2,500 per month (30,000 ÷ 12).

Given the resultant Net Cash and Overdraft Requirement figures, one might ask how Allan manages to have only an overdraft of 50,000 when the figures indicate that he never needs less than 60,000, except in December. There are two reasons. First, his mixture of cash and credit sales make averages notoriously inaccurate both in theory and in practice. Second, like most sensible business people, he delays his payments as long as reasonably possible (i.e. 45 days in practice as opposed to the theoretical 30). This is why a bank manager or equivalent always asks what the 'cash book' overdraft position is as well as the actual, purely to see how much extra credit is being 'fiddled'. In this case the difference between the overdraft used and the theoretical cash book one is normally less than 10 days' sales but in September, October and November the gap is such that a temporary overdraft increase is likely to be required.

In any event, September to November notwithstanding, Allan's business is one that the banks are normally very happy to see, despite the stream of poor results over the years. After all bookselling at this level is hardly a fashion or cyclical business and as long as people keep reading books there is little chance that the bank will do other than continue to collect its charges even though Allan is unlikely to ever make millions.

Comment

Twenty-five per cent margins, particularly with West End overheads to pay, are not conducive to high net profits. This tends to explain why there was such a rapid change in shop usage in areas like Soho when the 21-year leases negotiated just after the war started to expire and the old type of shops, relying primarily on local trade, could not hope to pay the vastly increased rents demanded. Allan's lease also runs out soon and whilst the covenant restricting usage to 'a bookshop' will help to mitigate against a totally unfeasible rent increase, only time will tell whether re-decorating the shop and concentrating on ever better service will enable him to survive, never mind flourish, particularly if a high bank rate adds other cost increases at the same time.

10

11   Growth

Theme: A discussion of the issues that arise when a small business grows

There are two problems relating to the growth of small businesses. The first is the effect on the organisation itself; the second, and in our view the more important, is the effect on the owners themselves.

Most small business people should know that the vast majority of small businesses that fail do so because they run out of cash. However, probably most of these small business people don't appreciate that the majority of these failures were *trading profitably* when they did crash, just like Rolls Royce.

Why can growing businesses fail?

Some of the major reasons for failure are simple ones:

1. *The big order*. This invariably requires new machinery, new staff, and perhaps more space. It certainly requires more materials and probably much more credit since big companies don't pay promptly. Hence the £100,000 order with a 50 per cent profit margin and a six month delivery time, is deadly if you have not worked out that you will need at least an *extra* £50,000 overdraft for no less than six months.
2. *The new salesperson* (extra staff). Try this addition: salary £10,000, plus NI contribution £2,000, plus car £10,000, plus expenses £2,000, *plus working capital on the extra sales* – say £50,000. Expensive aren't they!
3. *The new factory*. Hands up anyone who has ever moved house without spending a lot more money than you anticipated (you're right, the authors haven't either). Therefore, imagine the extra costs of moving business, particularly when you are already under tremendous pressure trying to meet all that extra business from overcrowded premises – which is why you need to move in the first place!
4. *Marginal costing*. Your costing system reveals that each item

produced costs £1 in materials and labour. You take an order to sell twice as many items as before at £1.20 thinking you are making 20p profit on every item. Unfortunately, the order means that you have to buy another machine at a *cost* of for example £10,000 to produce them. Moreover, you have not considered your own salary, the rent and all the other overheads. Moral: cost everything, not just *direct* materials and labour, then decide whether the extra order is worthwhile.

5. *Inherent inefficiencies of expansion.* It is one of the biggest myths of business that expansion always generates economies of scale. Despite such examples of the opposite as nationalised corporations, most people do not appreciate that the economies of scale rule applies only to certain industries – airlines and power generation for example. In general, commonsense should tell you it won't work for you! The more people you manage, the less time you can spend on each; the more customers and suppliers, the less time can be spent on each; the more machines, the less time is available to nurse them. An interesting example may convince you: a car engine with *every* part machined and set to 99 per cent perfect tolerances *will never work*.

6. *Competition.* It was the rabbit that stuck its head out of the hole that got its head blown off! The same applies to small business. Many small businesses can be making very nice profits indeed at a certain level of output and nobody cares. But expand and you start to encroach on other, usually bigger businesses', territory. The net result is invariably a 'price war'. Small businesses do *not* win price wars – their profits get squeezed and they have not got the long-term resources of the bigger competitor. Of course there are exceptions, but just remember not to 'back outsiders' without very careful thought.

Managing growth

Having said all this, the biggest overall cause of failure still lies with management itself. If you are a good manager and not just an effective small business person you will avoid most of the dangers by taking the following advice:

● You will always expand conservatively and carefully. Always stop and think it through.
● You will never link management objectives solely to *sales* but rather to *profitability*.

- You will have selected a good team to work with you.
- You will have already established a sound planning process to lay the foundation for *sustainable growth*. For example, you might well recruit a non-executive director to help you not only to plan but also to give *you* honest and unbiased advice and appraisal.
- You will have established a good management control and reporting system which is simple but effective. You can get it all on one A4 sheet per month.
- Be able to take corrective decisions early before your business gets out of control.
- Recognise that *profit margin and cashflow monitoring is vital*.
- Perhaps most importantly, according to Professor Sue Birley, establish an extensive network of friendships and contacts which can provide that crucial help in such areas as money, skills and markets.

This is all commendable in theory. In practice most businesses grow because they have to (the antique dealer and the bookshop) or because like Topsy 'they just grew and grew'. They do not grow simply because the masterplan decreed success, as Eastern Europe is currently discovering. Therefore, we would argue that it is essential for small business people to find out a lot more about themselves before they start on the treadmill.

Many people are sceptical about so-called psychometric testing – but there are many fewer when they've seen the results. We believe that they can be of significant use to the would-be entrepreneur. Primarily this is because they cause the business person to focus on what they are *really* like and not what they would *like* to be like.

It is both comic and revealing to see two groups, one of accountants and one of small business people, fill in a simple learning style inventory test. All stereotype characteristics of the 'carefully considering' accountant are revealed in full glory, usually much to their displeasure. Equally clearly revealed is the small business entrepreneur's approach of 'I know I can do it . . . what is this game of Russian roulette anyway'.

The problems come when, as occasionally happens, a so-called entrepreneur is revealed as having the learning style of an accountant or vice versa. The odds are that the accountant will not move into small business, but he may well move into a more exciting environment – Finance Director for Robert Maxwell perhaps! On the other hand the small business person can't become an accountant. What he or she does appear to do is worry infinitely more about the business than the average small business person. Moreover, they invariably spend endless hours on the monitoring and planning processes as they try desperately to lessen the 'risk' of being in such a precarious occupation as small business. They would probably prefer to be elsewhere, perhaps accountancy, to such an extent that some never even get started in small business — which is probably just as well. The relevance of this is simple: these people need 'entrepreneurs' in their team just as much as 'entrepreneurs' need accountants if both are to survive and prosper.

Without a combination of talents, the business might well start and possibly flourish in the short term but, as growth continues, cracks will appear. The moral here is: find out what type of person you are and build your growth team accordingly so that strengths and weaknesses are balanced.

A simple example is the managing director of a design company who, by using his own talents as a designer and using sub-contract labour, built up a nice little business to a £150,000 annual turnover. However, he never seemed to have enough time to find the new premises or the extra staff he knew he needed. We asked him to keep a diary for a fortnight. It revealed that, of the 140 hours he had worked (no Sundays), 80 hours were spent on the drawing board and a further 20 hours liaising directly with clients. After 25 hours were deducted for his time spent on administration it should be no surprise that he only spent two and a half hours 'managing' and two hours selling in the entire fortnight.

The diagnosis of his situation was:

- You are not a 'managing director'
- You need to recruit and train another 'doer' on the drawing board first and not an administrator as you thought.
- As leopards don't change spots, you probably need a part-time 'managing director' to organise and plan for both you and the business.

He is now sleeping at night for the first time in months having realised that it 'wasn't his fault'. Similarly many small business people forget that each business is indeed a triangle consisting of: sales, production and administration, as illustrated in Fig. 11.1.

When the business is small you can, just like the designer, do all these three functions, albeit specialising in one, by working all hours. As expansion proceeds what normally happens is that you take on a sales manager or production manager. Guess what happens to the invoicing and costing! The problem is, of course, made worse by the normal small business approach of paying as little as possible

Fig. 11.1

to everyone including yourself because the 'company can't afford it'. The net result of paying peanuts is invariably the employment of monkeys. This is a pity, especially if the 'monkey' is responsible for the costing and invoice system which is the basis of the business and which you are far too busy to check.

When you are working out whether you need extra help and are calculating how many hours *you* are working, remember to add 'worry time'. Some people can work 14-hour days and switch off instantly but most can't. Fourteen-hour days and two or three hours tossing and turning in bed is a guaranteed recipe for a nervous breakdown or a totally wrong yet critical business decision.

Finally, if you have no intention of being a tycoon and are perfectly content to be a one-man band or equivalent, great! You may not be very rich at the end of the day but contentment has its own rewards . . . or has it?

11

12 Some practical problems of growth

Theme: A case study illustrating some of the less obvious but vital issues concerned with growth

The previous chapter discussed the wide range of factors that affect the decision to grow or, if growth just happened, it pointed out possible sources of danger. We now go on to look at a case study which illustrates some of these problems. More importantly, it deals with a small but growing business at the very highest level of small business and demonstrates that the quest for finance can itself be a source of difficulty which can affect the very existence of the company. This being so, this case is, of course, the most complicated we have looked at.

To investigate the business we need to do some extra analysis but the simple methods we have used so far are still appropriate as a first step. Breakeven analysis, although simple, can be applied to complex financial problems in small business and a simple cashflow projection still provides most of the information we need.

Case 7: The engineer

Tom Baker and John Baron started in business as a partnership in 1977 producing specialised sheet metal fabrications, principally for the electronics business. Two years later the business had grown out of its original home, Tom's garden shed, and moved to a factory unit on a nearby industrial estate. During this period the company expanded significantly from its original £33,000 turnover but, despite efforts to broaden its customer range and number of products, by 1982 it still sold 80 per cent of its output to one major electronics company.

However by 1982, though still good friends, Tom and John dissolved the partnership, recognising that Tom's interest in increasingly sophisticated manufacturing methods as against John's traditional approach would mean long-term stress and future management problems.

Consequently Tom recruited a production manager to replace John and also recruited a finance director to keep the company on an even keel whilst he got on with developing his new product ideas, which involved the development of specialised frames for the computer industry. This development took over two years but in early 1985 a major computer company placed the first large order, subsequently increasing it substantially in May 1985. The value of that one order was just over £1 million.

In order to meet this contract Tom had to embark on a crash programme for the introduction of a totally new concept of manufacturing using CNC punching machines linked to a special computer design system, developed from scratch by himself and a nearby software company. This system enabled design, drawing and the use of raw material to be completed in one function thereby making new products and alterations to existing products a very fast and accurate process.

His new major customer was not the only one to be impressed. Demand for further design work and other sub-contract work increased rapidly. Tom's immediate reaction was to reorganise the company into three separate entities:

● A design company selling computerised manufacturing systems.
● A manufacturing company producing, specifically, the new products.
● A sub-contract company which was primarily the original manufacturing company. Whilst supplying the new manufacturing unit with its basic assemblies, it would remain separate.

Assets and liabilities were split accordingly and Tom was well pleased with his new empire. Or rather he was until Simon, his finance director, produced the budget forecasts for the new manufacturing company which was already gearing up to meet the £1 million plus contract. The first major deliveries from the supplemented work force of 85 were due in three months' time. Simon's figures were roughly as follows:

Balance Sheet	Now	A year's time
Debtors	22	200
Creditors	120	140
Fixed Assets (new machines)	250	220
Directors' Loans	45	45
Hire Purchase Commitment	100	70
Share Capital	10	10
Stocks	–	45
Overdraft	80	200

Profit and Loss

Sales	−	580
Cost of Sales	−	460
Overheads	−	200
Net Loss	55	80

NB 1. All figures are in £000
   2. The Cost of Sales of 460 are broken down:
      460 = 240 variable + 220 fixed
   3. The Overheads of 200 are broken down:
      40 variable costs + 160 fixed (including 35 finance costs,
      100 management salaries, pensions, etc.)

The figures told Simon that he would have to seek outside capital before the bank insisted upon it. Consequently, with the full support of their bankers, Tom and Simon approached a Merchant Bank who were also impressed by Tom's systems and large orders. They therefore offered the following deal (which we enclose in full for future benefit):

1. The Merchant Bank would purchase 25 per cent of the enlarged equity for £75,000 following conversion of the directors' loans (45,000) into ordinary shares.
2. The Merchant Bank would purchase 75,000 £1 convertible 10 per cent preference shares, the conversion rate of the preference shares to be based on pre-tax profits in respect of the year ended 1991 on the following scale:

Pre-Tax Profits	Additional Share of Equity on Conversion
Less than 150K	20%
150,000 – 200,000	15%
200,000 – 250,000	10%
250,000 and over	5%

   If profits failed to reach £150,000 in 1991, then at the Merchant Bank's option, the conversion period would be extended by two years to 1992. In the event of the bank not exercising their conversion rights the shares can be redeemed for £150,000. No dividend will be paid in the first year.
3. The company may not alter the auditors or accountants without the Merchant Bank's consent.
4. The Merchant Bank to have the right to appoint a non-executive director to the Board.

12

Please fill in your answers to questions 1 to 6. Each question tells you where to find help in case of difficulty.

1   Do you want to work in terms of units sold or money? If you have one product you will probably choose units sold. If you have more than one product you will probably choose money.

Please tick: Units sold

                 Money   ✓

2A   **Answer this question only if you ticked units sold in question 1. If you ticked money go on to question 2B.**
What is the selling price in £s?
      Please fill in the box.

      Price: £

What number of units do you expect to sell? (You can choose per week, per month or per year, but whatever time period you choose, you must keep to it for the rest of the analysis).
      Please fill in the box.

      Expected units sold:

Now go to question 3.

2B   **Answer this question only if you ticked money in question 1.**
What is you expected sales revenue, in £s? (You can choose per week, per month or per year, but whatever time period you choose, you must keep to it for the rest of the analysis).
      Please fill in the box.

      Expected Sales Revenue: £

Now go to question 4.

3   What are the variable costs per item, in £s?
      Please fill in the boxes.

	Amount	*Description*
Cost 1 £		
Cost 2 £		
Cost 3 £		
Cost 4 £		
Cost 5 £		
Cost 6 £		
Cost 7 £		
Cost 8 £		

4   What are the costs which are percentage of price or sales revenue?
      Please fill in the boxes.

	Percentage	Description
Cost 1	%	
Cost 2	%	
Cost 3	%	
Cost 4	%	

5   **Answer this question only if you ticked money in question 1. Otherwise go on to question 6.**
   Is there a cost in Profit Margin terms, e.g. when pricing is on a cost plus basis?

Profit Margin (9)	Description
107 %	Mark-up

6   What are the fixed costs, in £s? Make sure each cost covers the same time period, e.g. weekly, monthly, yearly.
   Please fill in the boxes.

	Amount	Description
Cost 1 £	220,000	From cost of sales
Cost 2 £	160,000	From overheads
Cost 3 £		
Cost 4 £		
Cost 5 £		
Cost 6 £		
Cost 7 £		
Cost 8 £		

The calculations
Pre-Calculations:

$$\frac{\text{Variable Costs}}{\text{Sales}} = \frac{280}{580}$$
$$= 0.78$$

$$\text{Contribution} = \text{Price} - \text{Variable Costs}$$
$$= 1.00 - 0.78$$
$$= 0.22$$

$$\text{Breakeven Point} = \frac{\text{Fixed Costs}}{\text{Contributions}}$$
$$= \frac{130}{0.22}$$
$$= 591$$

$$\text{Expected Profit} = (\text{Contribution} \times \text{Expected Sales}) - \text{Fixed Costs}$$

Fig. 12.1   Business viability chart for case 7

12

5. Board meetings will be held monthly. All minutes and board papers will be sent to the Merchant Bank.
6. The Merchant Bank will receive monthly management accounts within 10 working days of the end of each month.
7. The Merchant Bank to see and agree all budgets and operating plans for each financial year.
8. Key man insurance will be taken out for all directors for the benefit of the company at a value to be determined by the Merchant Bank.
9. The company to supply written details of the agreed salary scales for all directors and management.
10. The company to supply details of all bank loans and any other financing arrangements as well as written confirmation of the continuation and extent of overdraft facilities.
11. The company to meet all professional and legal fees incurred by the Merchant Bank in respect of the offer.
12. The company to pay a fee to the Merchant Bank of £2,500 on completion of the agreement.

This offer is subject to a legal contract. Please let us have a written response within 14 days.

The question is: do Tom and Simon have any choice?

Breakeven analysis

Like Case 6, whilst a loss situation is given, it is always worth checking; so we repeat our approach and find the contribution after the first year's trading. Of the 460 Cost of Sales, 280 were Variable Costs (240 from Cost of Sales, 40 from Overheads). Therefore:

$$\begin{aligned}
\text{Contribution} &= \text{Sales} - \text{Variable Costs} \\
&= 580 - 280 \\
&= 300 \\
&= 0.52 \text{ per £1 sales } \left(\frac{300}{580}\right)
\end{aligned}$$

The Fixed Costs are 380, made up of 220 from Cost of Sales and 160 from Overheads. Therefore:

$$\text{Breakeven} = \frac{\text{Fixed Costs}}{\text{Contribution}}$$

$$= \frac{380}{0.52}$$
$$= 730,000$$

Hence our calculations tally very closely with Simon's (see Fig. 12.1). The business is indeed scheduled to make a substantial loss at the budgeted sales turnover level.

In this situation the usual approach would be to expand sales or cut overheads or other direct costs. Unfortunately it is not a usual case. We already know that this factory had been designed to produce a specific product efficiently and that £580,000 sales in the context of a £1m plus order book represents probable capacity. Even more worryingly, one would anticipate, in a new factory producing new products to tight quality parameters, with an untrained work force, that Simon's figures are much more likely to be optimistic rather than pessimistic. Hence, most investors could look at a £100,000 loss as highly possible.

Alternatives? There are none! This is a perfectly normal situation for any business gearing up with new and invariably expensive technology and with a relatively inexperienced work force to produce a complex new product. The key, therefore, is to ensure the best possible management control over the production process and costs and, more importantly, not to run out of working capital whilst you are going through the learning curve (which is what happened to Rolls Royce as they geared up to make RB211 engines). As this sort of financing is not normally the province of the high street bank branches, Tom and Simon have indeed little choice if they want to become a major success.

Comment

Small Business Research in Manufacturing Business (David Storey *et al.*, 1987) reveals clearly that of every 100 manufacturing businesses formed just four produce *over half* the jobs created. This research indicates that these four can be spotted within the first two years. They have the following characteristics:

12

- It is generally three times as large, both in assets and employment, as its contemporaries.
- It is operating on lower gross profit margins than its rivals but retaining more of its profits.
- It is likely to be owned by experienced directors rather than being run as a family firm.

- It has started relatively large and is managed professionally.
- In the next few years its assets will not grow quickly but its work force will grow rapidly.

In other words, Tom's business fits the picture very nicely, which is another major reason why both the bank and the Merchant Bank were prepared to 'venture' accordingly.

It also illustrates the problem for any small business doing regular work for multi-nationals or their equivalent. Almost any order is likely to swamp your capacity and require rapid growth just to keep abreast of their requirements. This approach is thus fine for turnover and invariably fatal for short-term profit. Yet, if Tom does not reach £150,000 profit by 1991, the Merchant Bank stands to own 45 per cent of the company. Therefore, the bank cannot lose as long as the business survives and their monitoring system built into the deal makes survival at least easier to ensure.

Cashflow analysis

The second part of the investigation is to look at the company's cashflow situation. Recall that the finance director's figures were as follows at the end of the year:

Sales	580
Cost of Sales	460
Debtors	200
Overheads	200
Creditors	140
Stocks	45
Bank Overdraft	200
Reduction in Hire	
Purchase Commitment	30

NOTES:
1. The Cost of Sales of 460 are broken down:
   460 = 240 Variable + 220 Fixed
2. The Overheads of 200 are broken down:
   40 Variable Costs + 160 Fixed (including 35 Finance Costs, 100 management salaries, pensions, etc.)

Hence, in a similar way as before, you can fill in the cashflow chart. Firstly, sales at £580,000 for the year can be guessed to develop slowly as the new factory system gets up speed. July and August are

Cash Forecast

All figures in '000s	JAN	FEB	MAR	APR	MAY	JUN	JUL	AUG	SEP	OCT	NOV	DEC	TOTAL
SALES	20	30	40	50	55	60	50	50	60	65	65	35	580
SALES RECEIPTS	—	—	—	20	30	40	50	55	60	50	50	60	415
VARIABLE COSTS (usually purchases)	—	—	—	9.6	14.4	19.2	24.0	26.4	28.8	24.0	24.0	28.8	199.2
FIXED COSTS (usually overheads)	30	20.9	20.9	20.9	20.9	20.9	20.9	20.9	20.9	20.9	20.9	50.9	290
DIRECTORS' SALARY	10.0	10.0	10.0	10.0	10.0	10.0	10.0	10.0	10.0	10.0	10.0	10.0	120
NET CASH (cumulative) (sales less expenses)	(40)*	(70.9)	(101.8)	(122.3)	(137.6)	(147.7)	(152.6)	(154.9)	(154.6)	(159.5)	(164.4)	(194.1)	
OVERDRAFT REQUIREMENTS	40	75	105	125	140	150	155	155	155	160	165	200	

Fig. 12.2 Cashflow chart for case 7

* The brackets indicate a minus sign

12

bound to be affected by holidays and December is always affected badly. The result is the sales breakdown shown in Fig. 12.2.

Sales receipts are more complicated but, given that debts are expected to be £200,000 at the end of the year, it is not difficult to assume that Simon is basing his figures on a payment schedule of 90+ days. Therefore, January sales will be paid for in April, February's in May, etc., thus leaving October/November/December and half of September sales unpaid at the end of the year. This payment schedule would be normal from very big customers.

The Variable Cost element is difficult, but if the problem is taken in stages a feasible picture emerges. Firstly, we know from our previous calculations that Variable Costs total £280,000. By definition they vary with sales so that the ratio of variable cost to sales is 280/580 which is 48 per cent. It is also given that creditors at the end of the year will be £140,000. It can therefore be deduced that the company will pay its creditors every six months (280/140). In practice, some of its fixed costs can be delayed as well. However, it is normally unheard of to have credit periods of more than 90 days – at least in budgets! So, an assumption that variable costs will be paid at the same rate as sales receipts (i.e. three months +) is not unreasonable. The combination of a three months' lag and taking costs as 48 per cent of sales, enables the figure of 9.6 to be slotted into April, calculated from a sales figure in January of 20, and so on for the following months.

Fixed Costs are different from the amount used in the breakeven calculations, £380,000, because salaries are separated in the cashflow chart. We can calculate the new Fixed Costs figure as follows:

1. £380,000 from previous calculations
2. Subtract the £100,000 salary costs given in the accounts
3. Subtract a further amount for National Insurance which we are told was not included in the £100,000. At present rates this amounts to £20,000 (expensive isn't it!).

Fixed Costs = £260,000 (= 380 – 100 – 20)
Salary Costs = £120,000 (= 100 + 20)

Normally one would divide the £260,000 by the 12-month period and plug in the figure (£21,000). However, we are given one important figure, namely the opening overdraft of £40,000. As we can calculate the monthly salary figure simply as £10,000 (£120,000 ÷ 12 months) and as we also know that no Variable Costs will be paid in the first month, then the Fixed Cost figure must be

£30,000 (£40,000 overdraft − £10,000 salary bill). This is not unreasonable, bearing in mind that there are bound to be some costs incurred before the real start-up.

With one exception the rest of the Fixed Costs can therefore be assumed to be even throughout the year:

£20,900 per month (260 − 30 divided by 11).

The exception is December where, for sheer convenience, the 'missing' £30,000 of hire purchase commitment reduction can be slotted in, thus enabling the figures to balance with the stated ending overdraft of £200,000. Easy wasn't it!

Comment

It is perhaps predictable that within six months the company was in deep trouble and running out of cash again. The Merchant Bank called in a major accountancy firm to investigate. Their conclusions were as follows:

- The accuracy and adequacy of the present costing system relies primarily on the judgements made by Tom Baker. Independent verification of these costings is not possible.
- A less sophisticated but fully reconciled system would provide more comfort to the Board.
- The management accounts are of little practical use to management at present.

In other words, apart from Tom who designed this all-singing, all-dancing system, no one else has a clue what is going on except that it is losing money! Regrettably this is normal. Tom has lived, breathed and slept with his dream for many years and he is the last person to take the necessary overview and say, 'Let's make it much more simple and in control'. Simon, as the accountant, merely knows that the company is in trouble. He is not an engineer and consequently is bound to be treated as a lesser being (ironic for an accountant!) probably until it is too late and the company has run out of cash.

In reality, the facts of this case make a very fitting conclusion to this series of case studies. This is what happened:

- The Merchant Bank injected more money at a very high price. They insisted on management changes and the introduction of

12

a proper costing system (they should have done it before, of course!)

- Their big customer, hearing that they were in trouble, secretly investigated them in great depth and eventually offered to buy the company. The Merchant Bank was obviously delighted and agreed to sell. The big customer then withdrew its offer!
- With the offer withdrawn, the trade reputation of the company was compromised totally. It was squeezed by its trade creditors and the Merchant Bank. Its customers stopped giving orders (they didn't want to get key components caught in a bankruptcy either). Very shortly the receiver was called in.
- There was only one offer received by the receiver for the company as a whole. No prizes for guessing who! Their best customer bought it for a song, installed its own management and costing systems and went laughing all the way to the bank! Not only in literature do stories end 'et tu Brute'! The only redeeming feature of this case was that Tom had, if you remember, split his empire into three and he still had the other two, out of which he is still doing nicely – lucky, wasn't he!

13 And finally . . .

Theme: Think like a man of action and act like a man of thought

Let's now return to the process of small business start-ups and expansions which was first presented at the beginning of the book and is shown again in Fig. 13.1. The diagram (which does not include all tasks) shows where the main thrust of the book has been. We were trying to produce a simple picture as to whether the business is a starter or a non-starter and then, whether it can survive. This reveals automatically whether a business needs finance, and in what amounts. Simultaneously we have tried to remind you of the ever-present personal factors which can render these numbers pointless!

We have discussed whether the financial numbers 'look right' in some detail, and have illustrated the ideas with seven real-life detailed case studies. In doing so, we touched on many of the other issues shown in the diagram which are vital in running a small business. Of course no book can cover all these areas of interest to a level of detail appropriate to everybody's needs, but it is important that, having whetted your appetite, we can show you where to find extra help should you need it.

That is the purpose of this final chapter. However, there are very many sources of help of one kind or another and, rather than present an enormous list of books and agencies, we will restrict ourselves to just a few that we think you will find especially useful. These references will all have their own (sometimes very long) lists of references and can act as a lead-in to virtually every source of advice, finance or expertise you could possibly need. Before looking at the issues specifically mentioned in Fig. 13.1, you should be aware that there are many, many sources of free general advice.

General advice

There are 30 agencies giving advice and support to small businesses in London alone. In the whole of the UK there are more than 350. How do you choose between them? With difficulty; but you should start with NatWest's booklet *Start Up and Go* and the government's

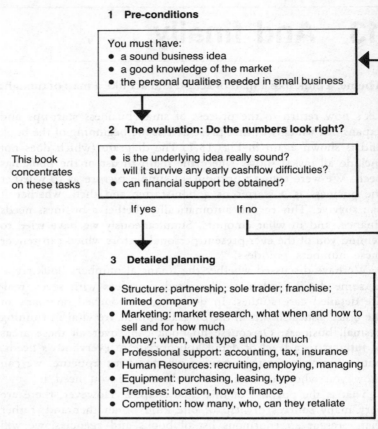

1   Pre-conditions

You must have:
- a sound business idea
- a good knowledge of the market
- the personal qualities needed in small business

2   The evaluation: Do the numbers look right?

This book concentrates on these tasks

- is the underlying idea really sound?
- will it survive any early cashflow difficulties?
- can financial support be obtained?

If yes   If no

3   Detailed planning

- Structure: partnership; sole trader; franchise; limited company
- Marketing: market research, what when and how to sell and for how much
- Money: when, what type and how much
- Professional support: accounting, tax, insurance
- Human Resources: recruiting, employing, managing
- Equipment: purchasing, leasing, type
- Premises: location, how to finance
- Competition: how many, who, can they retaliate

Fig. 13.1   Starting up and expanding a small business

Small Business Service. The latter will give three consultations free of charge.

In London, *Getting Started*, published by LENTA, gives an excellent introduction.

References

1. *Start Up and Go*, NatWest. Available from any branch.
2. Small Business Service, Ebury Bridge House, Ebury Bridge Road, London SW1W 8QD. 071-730 8451 or Freefone Enterprise.
3. *Starting Up* by Gary Jones, Pitman.
4. *Getting Started*, LENTA, 4 Snowhill, London EC1. 071-236 3000.

Pre-conditions

A sound business idea

We have shown you how to evaluate a business idea: Is it viable? Will it survive? If you want to get into small business but lack a business idea in the first place then your problem is much more basic. However, there are books and agencies to help generate ideas and the main ones are listed in *Getting Started* or *Start Up and Go*.

Reference

Getting Started (page 2), LENTA, London.
Start Up and Go, NatWest.

A good knowledge of the market

There are three essential questions you must ask, whatever the product or service you are trying to sell.

- Who are the customers, or potential customers?
- What, exactly, do they want?
- How will you beat the competition?

The answers will depend upon the business idea you have in mind but unless you can give plausible answers you shouldn't start, at least until you have thought through the idea more carefully. This stage does not call for elaborate market research, just the basics of whether your idea, however good, is an idea capable of being turned into a profitable business.

The best help is from your friends and acquaintances. What do they think? You should also try a few spot checks such as those suggested for Harry's Fish and Chip shop in Chapter 4.

Personal qualities

The case studies should have convinced you that not everybody is cut out to run a small business. You may prefer to sleep well rather than eat well. If you haven't a suitable psychological make-up perhaps you should forget it and take a course in banking or accountancy. If you're not sure, or want confirmation that you are a potential 'small business person', then there are guides to help you and assessment tests you can take. *The Entrepreneur's Complete Self-Assessment*

13

Guide has advice, backed up by three quizzes, to help you assess your entrepreneurial and management skills.

Reference

The Entrepreneur's Complete Self-Assessment Guide by Douglas A. Gray, Kogan Page.

Detailed planning

All the aspects of detailed planning that we show in Fig. 13.1 are excellently described and explained in Gary Jones's book *Starting Up*. He covers Market Research, Human Resources, Equipment, Premises and Competition much better than we could and so we suggest you consult this book when you reach the detailed planning stage. However, some of the topics are so important that we feel compelled to mention them in outline here.

Reference

Starting Up, by Gary Jones, Pitman.

Business plans

Whilst Alan West's *A Business Plan* in the NatWest Small Business Bookshelf series advises the small business person how to write a full business plan in exhaustive detail, it is not always necessary. Just like the NatWest 'cashflow' chart was a useful check list, so is Alan's book. Hence, if you can get the key points about your business idea on to two pages of A4 – fine. Particularly if the business idea involves less than £10,000 to start with, the concept of three-year Profit and Loss accounts and Balance sheets is, frankly, nonsense. So remember, 'keep it simple, keep it honest' is far better advice and more useful than 50 pages of verbal overkill.

Legal structure

Having established that your business could possibly work, the next issue to tackle is its structure. If you are going into business with other people this issue could cause you more ulcers than your cashflow and bank manager combined. The Lawyers for Enterprise Scheme will give an initial consultation free of charge. However, you may be better to start with one of the agencies that give advice for small businesses. It will include basic legal advice amongst its services. You can find addresses in *Start Up and Go* but, since many of the agencies are locally based, you should also ask at your local library.

References

1. The Lawyers for Enterprise Scheme, The Law Society, 113 Chancery Lane, London WC2A 1PL.
2. *Start Up and Go*, NatWest.

Money

This book should have helped you find out whether you need finance, how much you need and how to use it when you get it. But, where do you get it? In broad terms the sources are:

1. *Clearing banks.* All major clearing banks are courting small businesses. However, the service and support they give varies. Try your local banks and see which one makes the best initial impression.
2. *Local government.* Ask at your local library for addresses, or consult the 'NatWest's Business Information Bureau' which lists sources of help and finance by geographical areas.
3. *National government.* In particular find out more about the Enterprise Allowance Scheme and the Loan Guarantee Scheme from the Small Business Service or your local Job Centre.
4. *Other agencies, trusts.* If you don't like the banks and government authorities, there is an enormously wide range of other sources. For a selected list of some of the main ones see *Start Up and Go.* For what seems to be a comprehensive list of around 160 sources of small business finance, try *Working for Yourself.*
5. *The Prince's Trust.* If you are young or unwaged, obtaining finance can be much more difficult because you have neither collateral nor a track record. However, there are agencies specialising in finance for young people. In particular, the Prince's Trust is the most used body providing advice and finance for small business start-ups. They offer advice and money to people under 26 with a firm business idea. However, there are a few tips which we think you may find useful:

   (a) Parents may not be prepared to fund your small business

13

but they may be prepared to guarantee your overdraft, particularly if you give them a professional presentation before visiting the bank.

(b) It is not difficult to raise *some* capital (say £1,000) by working at weekends or evenings or, perhaps more usefully, by helping out at any of the many street markets scattered around the country.

(c) *Any* job, even a paper round, can give you some credibility with a bank. If the newsagent can say: 'Yes, he/she is highly reliable and can be left near the till', then this is valuable information to the bank manager.

(d) If at first you don't succeed, don't give up and blame the government etc. Not only is it not truly their fault, but also it will not get you into a positive state of mind.

6. *Venture capital.* For larger amounts you are moving into the area of venture capital. Most clearing banks have venture capital divisions and associations with venture capitalists. However, for an independent view, the British Venture Capital Association provides a full list of venture capitalists and advice on how to choose between them. But remember 'The Engineer' case study and be warned!

References

1. 'Business Information Bureau', NatWest.
2. Prince's Youth Business Trust, 5 The Pavement, London SW4 0HY. 071-498 3939.
3. *Working for Yourself* by Godfrey Golzen, Daily Telegraph.
4. British Venture Capital Association, etc.

Professional support

The chapters on bank managers and accountants will have given you guidance on what to look for. For a bank manager you should try your local branches, after first asking around other small business people who may have first-hand experience of the quality, or otherwise, of service.

Asking around will also be a good source of information about accountants but, for an overall view, try one of the accounting institutes who will be able to give you names of accountants practising in your area and may even be able to give guidance as to which of them might specialise in your type of business.

You will not, necessarily, require a lawyer and your first port of call should be one of the agencies or trusts giving general advice, such as those mentioned in *Start Up and Go* or *Getting Started*. On the other hand the 'Lawyers for Enterprise Scheme' will give more specialised assistance.

References

1. The Lawyers for Enterprise Scheme, The Law Society, 113 Chancery Lane, London WC2A 1PL.
2. *Start Up and Go*, NatWest.
3. *Getting Started*, LENTA.

Final comment

Please remember some of the commonest mistakes and avoid them.

- Business partners are like marriage partners. Pick a wrong one and it can be very expensive even if not fatal. A lengthy courtship is advised!
- The time to worry is when you are doing really well. Remember 'The Engineer'.
- It is never a sin to have 1001 ideas and not proceed with any of them (because you will always think up some more). The crime is to 'marry' the first idea that comes along, at least without processing it *very* carefully.
- Never go into business without a bank manager or accountant with whom you get on really well.
- Do not persevere in small business even though you hate it, just because the big companies you have previously worked for did not suit.
- If your sales exceed your stock by more than a factor of 10 (e.g. £10,000 stock, £100,000 sales) start to panic for you are about to either (a) blow a business fuse, or (b) prove you're cleverer than Tesco.
- It is dangerous in the extreme to congratulate yourself when having bought, for example, 100 items, you have sold 60 at 100 per cent profit in a short space of time. You must remember that the calculation of your profit margins *must* include the other 40 items still in stock. You may find that they are unsaleable.
- Never buy a Rolls Royce or Porsche before the business *really can* afford it!

13

Appendix

Blank viability chart

You are permitted to photocopy this for your own use but not for sale or distribution.

Please fill in your answers to questions 1 to 6. Each question tells you where to find help in case of difficulty.

1   Do you want to work in terms of units sold or money? If you have one product you will probably choose units sold. If you have more than one product you will probably choose money.

Please tick: Units sold

Money

2A   **Answer this question only if you ticked units sold in question 1. If you ticked money go on to question 2B.**
What is the selling price in £s?
Please fill in the box.

Price: £

What number of units do you expect to sell? (You can choose per week, per month or per year, but whatever time period you choose, you must keep to it for the rest of the analysis).
Please fill in the box.

Expected units sold:

Now go to question 3.

2B   **Answer this question only if you ticked money in question 1.**
What is you expected sales revenue, in £s? (You can choose per week, per month or per year, but whatever time period you choose, you must keep to it for the rest of the analysis).
Please fill in the box.

Expected Sales Revenue: £

Now go to question 4.

3   What are the variable costs per item, in £s?
Please fill in the boxes.

	Amount	Description
Cost 1 £		
Cost 2 £		
Cost 3 £		
Cost 4 £		
Cost 5 £		
Cost 6 £		
Cost 7 £		
Cost 8 £		

4   What are the costs which are percentage of price or sales revenue?
Please fill in the boxes.

	Percentage	Description
Cost 1	%	
Cost 2	%	
Cost 3	%	
Cost 4	%	

5   **Answer this question only if you ticked money in question 1. Otherwise go on to question 6.**
Is there a cost in Profit Margin terms, e.g. when pricing is on a cost plus basis?

Profit Margin	Description
%	

6   What are the fixed costs, in £s? Make sure each cost covers the same time period, e.g. weekly, monthly, yearly.
Please fill in the boxes.

	Amount	Description
Cost 1 £		
Cost 2 £		
Cost 3 £		
Cost 4 £		
Cost 5 £		
Cost 6 £		
Cost 7 £		
Cost 8 £		

The calculations
Contribution = Price − Variable Costs

$$\text{Breakeven Point} = \frac{\text{Fixed Costs}}{\text{Contributions}}$$

Expected Profit = (Contribution × Expected Sales) − Fixed Costs

Appx

Fig. A.1

Index

accountants, 19–24
advice (government etc.), 101
antique dealer case, 37–40, 71–3
Archimedes, 77

Balance Sheet, 90
bank charges, 19
banks and bankers, 8–18
bookshop case, 54–60, 78–81
breakeven analysis, 2, 24–60, 89, 94–5
breakeven point, 25, 39, 45, 51, 56
Business Information Bureau, 1
business plans, 104
Business Viability Chart, 41, 60, Figs. 8.1, 8.2, 12.1

Capital Radio, ix
car running costs, 33
cashflow, 61–81
cashflow analysis, 2, 96
cashflow forecast, 65–81, 96–7, Figs. 9.1, 9.2
contribution, 26
credibility, 4, 105–6
credit periods, 74–7

depreciation, 33, 35, 73
driving instructor case, 32–5, 69–71

engineer case, 89–100
enterprise allowance scheme, 6
entrepreneurs, 1, 15, 86, 103–4
export credit guarantees, 77
exporter case, 49–54, 74–8

factory, 77–8
failures, 83–4
fashion business, 14
'Firmstart', ix, 3
Fish and Chip shop case, 26, 32, 41, 65, Fig. 7.1
fixed costs, 25, 31, 39, 45, 50, 56, 65–81, 90–4, 98

growth, 41, 83–100, 101
guarantees, 16, 18

hi-tech business, 14

'key' numbers, 65

lease-purchase, 77
legal advice, 104 – 6
lemmings, 2
loan, 15
London Business School, ix

management, 84
management control system, 85
marginal costing, 83
market, 103
market trader case, 73 – 4
merchant banks, 91 – 6, 99

NatWest Growth Option, 15
net book agreement, 55
net cost, 66, 67
non-executive director, 55, 85

overdrafts, 15, 17

partners, 54 – 60, 89
percentage of sales costs, 31
planning, 104
Premium Bonds, 78
Prince's Trust, 105, 106
Profit & Loss, 91
'profit margin' cost, 31
profitability, 84
psychometric testing, 85

redundancy deal, 49, 68
risk, 12, 13, 14, 25, 56
Rolls Royce, 61, 95

seasonality, 73 – 4
'seed-corn' (NatWest), 15
shop, 28, 29, 68, 80 – 1
small business advisors, 11
starting up, x, 4, 101
stock-turn, 38

unit costs, 31

variable cost, 26, 31, 38, 45, 50, 55, 65 – 81, 90 – 4, 98
VAT, 19
venture capital, 106
viability, 4, 25 *et seq.*

'worry time', 87

Still not sure whether your business proposal is viable?

What you need is . . .

The Viability Program

This program, developed specifically to go with this book, has been written, tested and found to be User Friendly for any small business person. *Viability* asks you questions about your business idea and can give you the answers – clearly, accurately and in full colour.

Its advantage for anyone owning an IBM compatible computer is that it can do all the calculations to test the viability of your business very, very quickly. You are then given the opportunity to change your financial, marketing and business assumptions when you like, enabling you to explore why the idea appears successful or not. Moreover, *Viability* comes complete with 'Help' screens at every stage to allow even the most innumerate to produce a sensible scenario of their chances.

Price £29.95, including postage and packing.

Write, enclosing cheque (made out to Jayboon Ltd) or postal order to:

John Lambden
9 Church Street
ST IVES
Cambridgeshire
PE17 4DG